INSIGHT POCKET GUIDE

KU-265-105

FLORENCE

APA PUBLICATIONS

Part of the Langenscheidt Publishing Group

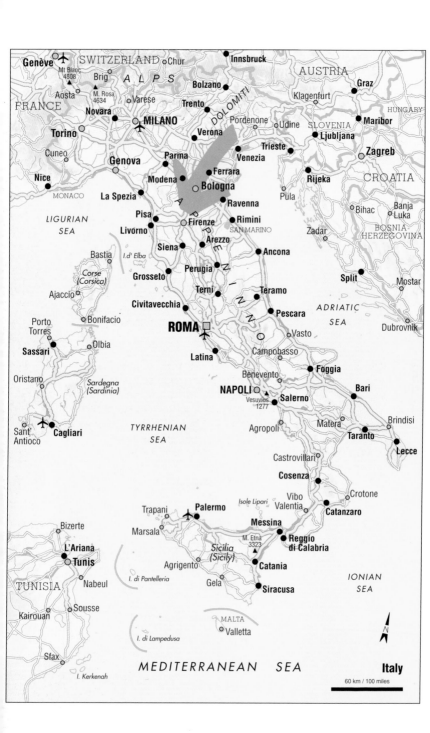

Italy

60 km / 100 miles

Welcome

This guidebook combines the interests and enthusiasms of two of the world's best-known information providers: Insight Guides, who have set the standard for visual travel guides since 1970, and Discovery Channel, the world's premier source of non-fiction television programming. Its aim is to bring you the best of Florence and its surroundings in a series of tailor-made itineraries designed by Christopher Catling, Insight's regular writer on Florence and the Tuscany region.

The author shows visitors how to make the best use of a short stay in the city. The first three tours link the essential sights, such as the Duomo, the Uffizi gallery, the Ponte Vecchio and the Pitti Palace; they each take a day to complete. The remaining city itineraries, aimed at visitors with more time, focus on other interesting areas and aspects of Florence, exploring worthwhile museums, churches and *palazzos* (with dips into markets and gardens), including a bus ride to nearby Fiesole. Lastly there is an Excursions section with recommended day trips to Pisa and Lucca by train. Supporting the itineraries are sections on history and culture, shopping, eating out, nightlife, festivals and practical information.

Christopher Catling first went to Florence as an art historian, at a time when his taste in art was aggressively pro-modern and he did not believe anything painted before Van Gogh could hold any interest for him, especially not religious art. But Florence taught him how wrong he could be, for he quickly developed a passion for Renaissance art. One of his main aims in *Insight Pocket Guide: Florence* has been to provide a painless introduction to the city's wealth of art and architecture, in the hope of persuading others to take the very same journey as himself – 'from relative ignorance to relative enlightenment'.

6   **contents**

Pages 2/3: view from the dome of the Duomo
Pages 8/9: Ponte Santa Trinità

History &Culture

The year 1401 marks a watershed in the history of Western civilisation. That was the year in which Florence's wool merchants' guild, the Arte di Calimala, announced that it would sponsor an artist to make new bronze doors for the city's baptistry. The aim was to rival the doors of Pisa's cathedral. Five artists were asked to make a bronze relief illustrating the story of Abraham and Isaac. The judges shortlisted the candidates to two – Lorenzo Ghiberti and Filippo Brunelleschi, whose panels are now displayed in the Bargello Museum *(see Itinerary 4, page 45)*. Scholars continue to argue over their respective merits. The prize was awarded to Ghiberti but modern critics tend to prefer Brunelleschi's more dramatic treatment.

Both works were revolutionary; the bronze reliefs demonstrated a new concern for realism, and also conveyed the emotive force of the biblical paradigm. In rejecting the iconographic formalism of medieval art and looking back to classical Greek and Roman art for inspiration, the panels represent a major shift in the history of artistic expression. The Renaissance had begun.

Florentine art of the 15th century was also indebted to the Etruscans, who pre-dated the Romans by several centuries. Rising above Florence towards Fiesole you can see the remains of an Etruscan town whose huge stone walls were laid in the 7th century BC. The Etruscans thrived as traders for 300 years; the cause of their demise remains something of a mystery.

The Etruscan city was Fiesole: Florence was founded in 59 BC, when it was established as a *colonia* for retired Roman soldiers. The name *Florentia* could be a reference to the wild flowers that grow in the Arno plain and on the surrounding hillsides, or it could mean 'destined to flourish'. The Romans who settled the city were devoted to the Horatian/Virgilian ideal of *rus in urbe* – the countryside in the town. The marriage of nature and necessity survived down the centuries. Many travellers admired the chapel-in-the-woods atmosphere of the city's 12th- and 13th-century Romanesque churches.

Europe's Richest City

The city has traditions of trailblazing commerce and political independence. In the 11th century, Florentine merchants began importing wool from northern Europe and rare dye-stuffs from the Mediterranean and the east. They developed specialised weaving and dyeing techniques that made the wool trade the city's main source of income: by 1250 the industry employed about a third of the city's inhabitants. By the 14th century Florence was Europe's richest city.

Left: Florence in the 15th century
Right: woodcut of Florentine bankers

The Renaissance was not created by Ghiberti and Brunelleschi – their art reflected the prevailing mood. And it would not have been possible without the patronage of wealthy Florentine individuals and religious foundations. The city's merchants invented credit banking, and the city's florin became the first common European currency, widely accepted and circulated because of the purity of its gold content.

Dante, who was born in Florence in 1265 and exiled on false charges of corruption in 1302, derided the city as a 'glut of self-made men and quick-got gain'. The Florentines' nascent capitalism may have been distasteful to Dante, but it fuelled the city's transformation in the 15th and 16th centuries. The old city, whose skyline bristled with defensive towers, was torn down in favour of new, classically inspired *palazzi* (palaces). Civic pride was expressed in new churches, libraries, monasteries, hospitals and orphanages, some financed by guilds or private patrons, others by public taxation.

The new buildings provided numerous commissions for artists, many of whom were architect, engineer, painter, sculptor and bronze-caster combined. They wanted to create art that reflected the confident spirit of the age; rejecting the stylised religious art of the preceding era they looked to nature and to antiquity for their models and subject matter.

The World's Biggest Dome

Innovations came thick and fast. Brunelleschi built the vast, gravity-defying dome that crowns the cathedral. Inspired by the ancient Roman Pantheon, he constructed what was then the world's largest dome. Soaring above a sea of terracotta roof tiles, the dome has come to symbolise the city. New depths of realism were achieved by Donatello, whose statue of St George, made for the guild of armourers in 1416 (now in the Bargello Museum – *see Itinerary 4, page 45*), is a superb

Above: bronze relief on the Baptistry door
Left: the gravity-defying dome

portrait of courage tempered by anxiety. Even more startling is his bronze figure of *David* (also in the Bargello), completed in 1440 – the first realistic nude in art since antiquity and one that paved the way for Michelangelo's renowned version of the same subject.

Masaccio blazed a new trail in the technique of perspective in 1425 with his frescoes on the *Life of St Peter*, in Santa Maria del Carmine *(see Itinerary 3, page 43)*, and his precise geometry was rapidly adopted by other artists. Technical innovations underlay many artistic achievements: Luca della Robbia perfected the art of glazed terracotta (see his roundels on the facade of the Innocenti orphanage – *see Itinerary 5, page 47*) and kept the technique a secret, known only to his family, who thereby enriched themselves mightily.

Other artists developed new paint pigments, which accounts for the amazing range and brilliance of the colours in the frescoes and paintings of artists as diverse as Botticelli (the Uffizi – *Itinerary 1, page 29*), Gozzoli (the Medici-Riccardi Palace – *Itinerary 2, page 34*), and Pontormo (Santa Felicità church – *Itinerary 3, page 39*). Above all, the towering genius of Michelangelo is evident in his huge, heroic and elemental sculptures.

The Medici Family

The Medici family ruled Florence almost continuously from 1434 until 1737. Their coat of arms (six red balls on a field of gold beneath a ducal coronet) can be seen all over Florence and Tuscany. Some say the balls represent medicinal pills and that the name Medici suggests descent from apothecaries. Others say the discs represent money and are a symbol of the bank founded by Giovanni di Bicci de' Medici (1360–1429) at the start of the 15th century. The bank expanded rapidly and was entrusted with the collection of papal revenues, laying the foundation of the family fortune.

The first of the family to become actively involved in political life was Giovanni's son, Cosimo de' Medici. Though he never sought public office, he proved an able behind-the-scenes manipulator. Cosimo, and subsequently his grandson, Lorenzo ('the Magnificent'), used their diplomatic skills to bring an end to the costly and inconclusive wars with rival cities that had brought Florence to the verge of bankruptcy. Both thereby helped to create the relatively prosperous and peaceful environment that enabled the city to give birth, simultaneously, to the Renaissance and to humanism.

The humanists shared an interest in classical philosophy and ideas. The humanist Aeneas Sylvius Piccolomini became Pope Pius II, although the humanistic emphasis on reason, knowledge and the centrality of man

Right: Eleonora of Toledo, wife of Cosimo I, with her son, Giovanni de' Medici

was hardly compatible with much of the contemporary Christian dogma.

Cosimo de' Medici, the humanist circle's patron, paid for scholars to come to Florence to teach Latin and Greek, and also funded the travels of Poggio Bracciolini, who tracked down lost manuscripts, including the works of Cicero, Lucretius and Quintilian. A huge number of precious works were copied, translated and keenly discussed. Some were housed in the public library attached to the monastery of San Marco, others in the Laurentian Library *(see Itinerary 2, page 34)*. Classical ideas rapidly fed through to artists who, already inspired by ancient art and architecture, now faced demands for pictures of mythological, historical and secular subjects – no longer was art exclusively concerned with religious themes.

'The New Rome'

Cosimo died in 1464 leaving Florence prosperous, peaceful and with just claim to the title 'the New Rome'. His son, Piero, did not survive for long. In 1469, Lorenzo de' Medici took over. He was a worthy successor: he had absorbed his grandfather's humanism, and he was a renowned poet who promoted the study of Dante, Boccaccio and Petrarch in the schools of Florence, thus ensuring that the Tuscan or Florentine dialect, in which these men wrote, would become the standard for written and spoken Italian. Until then it had been unthinkable to read or write in anything other than Latin.

Lorenzo was equally talented as a statesman. He did much to heal old enmities among the rival city states of northern Italy, encouraging the most powerful to form a defensive alliance against the territorial ambitions of France's Charles VIII. When he died in 1492, Pope Innocent VIII declared, with great foresight, 'The peace of Italy is at an end.'

Florence was left leaderless; Lorenzo's son, Piero de' Medici, succeeded him but when, in 1494, Charles VIII invaded Italy and marched on Florence, Piero surrendered the city and fled. Savonarola, a firebrand preacher, stepped into the vacuum, and convinced his fellow Florentines that the city was being punished by God for its profane art and pagan philosophies. He framed a republican constitution, founded on strict religious principles, and presided over a brief reign of terror during which petty misdemeanours were punished by torture; the streets blazed with 'bonfires of vanities' on which mirrors, books, art, musical instruments and fine clothing – all regarded as ungodly – were burnt.

Savonarola was eventually excommunicated by the pope. Tortured until he pleaded guilty to heresy, he was hanged in 1498 – a fire was then lit round the scaffold in Piazza della Signoria.

Left: Lorenzo de' Medici, statesman and poet

For a short period the republic was ruled by Piero Soderini and his infamous chancellor, Niccolò Machiavelli, but the Medicis were determined to regain control of the city. This was not exactly an onerous task given that Lorenzo de' Medici's second son was crowned Pope Leo X in 1513. Leo X entered the city in triumph in 1515 and Machiavelli, after a period of imprisonment, retired to write *Il Principe (The Prince)*, his famous reflections on the art of war and the dirty world of realpolitik.

Michelangelo the Defender

Florence attempted to regain its independence in 1530. Michelangelo was put in charge of the city's defences, manning the barricades around the church of San Miniato, high above the city of Florence, in a doomed attempt to repel the combined forces of the Medicis, the pope and the Holy Roman Emperor. Having supervised temporary fortifications and the hasty construction of an artillery platform around the tower of the church, Michelangelo then fled – behaviour that was later attributed to his 'artistic temperament' and therefore not held against him.

After stout resistance, the city fell to the Medicis. Alessandro de' Medici was crowned Duke of Florence, the first in a series of Medici dukes who proved corrupt, debauched and tyrannical. He was murdered by his cousin, Lorenzaccio, and succeeded by Cosimo I, a ruthless ruler who first set about destroying all his opponents in Florence, then systematically conquering rival cities, such as Siena, to carve out the Grand Duchy of Tuscany. Cosimo's 'achievements' were recorded by Vasari, whose vainglorious frescoes can be seen in the Palazzo Vecchio *(see Itinerary 1, page 28)*. Vasari also built the Uffizi for him *(Itinerary 1, page 29)*.

Cosimo I's aggressive leadership forced Tuscany into political unity and brought a new stability to the region, which thereafter played a relatively minor role in European history.

Above: interior courtyard of the Palazzo Vecchio

It was not long before the great artists deserted the city, in what Mary McCarthy, author of *The Stones of Florence*, has called 'the great diaspora of artistic talent'. Florence ceased to be the centre of artistic excellence, and for the great achievements of the High Renaissance we must look elsewhere – to Rome and Venice for example.

It is ironic that this second Cosimo de' Medici presided over a decline in the arts, whereas his predecessors, had played such a vital role in their encouragement. His successors, who nominally ruled Florence for another six generations, contributed little, either to government or the arts. The dynasty finally expired with the death of Anna Maria in 1743.

Grand Tourists

In the 19th century, as people began to appreciate the achievements of the 'pre-Raphaelite' artists, Florence started to become the tourist destination that it is today, renowned for its awesome heritage of 15th- and 16th-century art. It became a station on the Grand Tour, for aristocratic dilettantes and members of the literati and later for the increasingly rich and adventurous middle classes of Europe and America.

Today, Florence is a busy working town that balances the needs of residents and the demands made upon the city by the 8 million visitors who arrive annually. For at least six months of the year, Florence can be quite unpleasantly overcrowded, with long queues for every museum. Precious monuments are showing visible signs of erosion.

Tourist board officials and the mayor have proposed charging visitors to enter Florence, calling the whole city an 'open-sky museum'. It is only fair, they argue, that those who visit the city should contribute to its upkeep. Others want to go even further and limit the numbers of visitors by making them book in advance. Such measures sound drastic, but many locals feel that they are the only way to restore their quality of life and give Florence back its *vivabilita* – liveability.

Above: taking a break in the Piazza del Duomo

HISTORY HIGHLIGHTS

59BC Foundation of the Roman colony of Florentia.

AD250 The martyrdom of St Minias, to whom a shrine is dedicated on the site of San Miniato church. This is the first evidence of Christianity in Florence.

4th century Building of Santa Reparata, the city's first cathedral. Its ruins survive in the Duomo (cathedral) crypt.

1125 Florence conquers and destroys neighbouring Fiesole.

13th century Embroiled in factional conflicts, Florence sides with the Guelf (pro-pope) party against Ghibelline (pro-emperor) cities, such as Pisa and Siena.

1260 Siena defeats Florence at the battle of Montaperti but is dissuaded from destroying the city.

1302 Dante, a victim of the Guelf conflict, is expelled from Florence, whereupon he begins to write *The Divine Comedy*.

1322 Completion of the Palazzo Vecchio.

1348 The Black Death rages through Europe and kills three-fifths of the Florentine population over the next 50 years. The catastrophic effects of the plague in Florence inspire Boccaccio to write his *Decameron*.

1384 The Florentines capture Arezzo.

1400–1401 A competition is held to design new doors for the baptistry – an event regarded by art historians as the start of the *rinascita* (rebirth) or Renaissance.

1406 Florence conquers Pisa and gains a sea port.

1434 Cosimo de' Medici returns from exile to establish the city as an artistic and intellectual centre.

1469 Cosimo's grandson Lorenzo ('the Magnificent') de' Medici assumes power, aged 20.

1494 Savonarola declares Florence a republic ruled only by God.

1498 Execution of Savonarola.

1512 Florence is defeated by invading Spanish army, which facilitates the return of the Medicis.

1527 Florence expels the Medicis once again, and returns to its republican constitution.

1530 Pope Clement VII and Emperor Charles V join forces and their armies besiege Florence.

1531 Florence falls.

1555 Start of Cosimo I's campaign to reunite Tuscany by force.

1570 Cosimo I is appointed Grand Duke of Tuscany.

1610 Cosimo II appoints Galileo as court mathematician.

1631 Galileo is excommunicated.

1737 The last Medici grand duke dies without an heir and the title passes to the Austrian House of Lorraine.

1808 France annexes Tuscany.

1848 Tuscany serves as the vanguard in the first Italian War of Independence.

1865 Florence becomes the temporary capital of the emerging united Italy.

1919 Benito Mussolini founds the Italian Fascist Party.

1944 The Nazis destroy parts of central Florence. The Ponte Vecchio is the only old bridge to survive World War II.

1946 Italy becomes a republic.

1966 Florence is flooded by the River Arno and many works of art are lost. The disaster leads to a massive programme of restoration.

1988 Florentines vote to exclude traffic and to control air pollution.

1993 A Mafia bomb kills five people and damages the Uffizi gallery.

1998 Toto Riina and other Mafia figures are given life sentences for the Uffizi bombing.

2001 In a bid to end long queues, major museums such as the Uffizi introduce a pre-booking system, allowing for immediate entry at fixed arrival times.

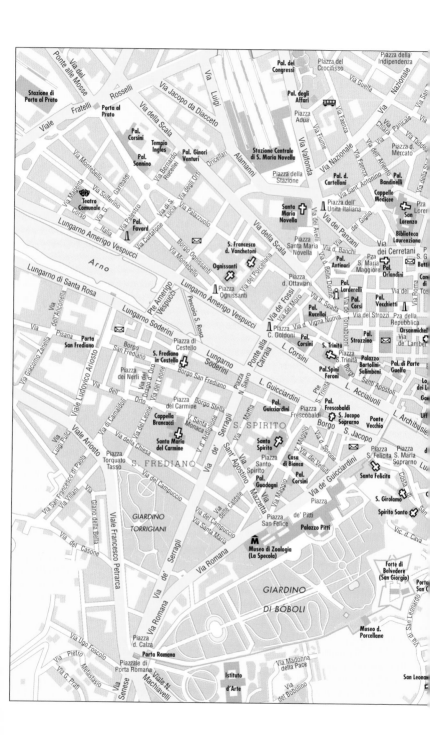

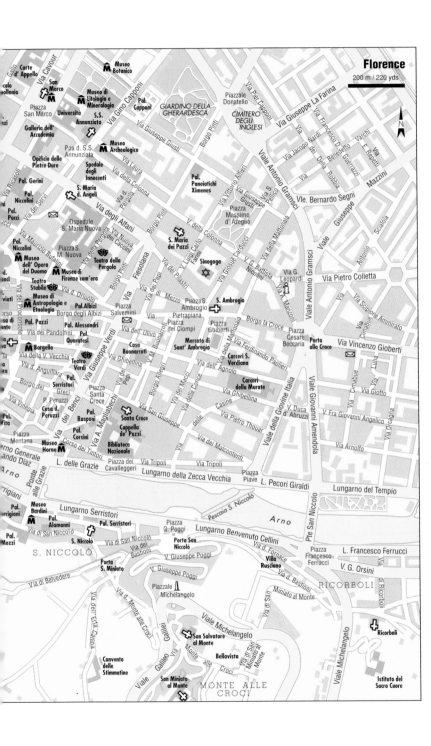

Orientation

The *centro storico*, the historic centre of Florence, is very compact and can be crossed on foot in less than half an hour. Strolling through the maze of mostly medieval streets is a real pleasure. You are not likely to get lost, since certain landmarks – the great dome of the cathedral and the tower of the Palazzo Vecchio – can be seen from afar, and most of the streets are oriented north–south or east–west. Via dei Calzaiuoli (Shoemakers' Street) is the city's spine, a broad pedestrian street connecting the Duomo to the Piazza della Signoria where the Palazzo Vecchio has been the City Hall since 1296. The colonnades of the Uffizi Gallery begin here, forming a walkway called the Piazzale degli Uffizi stretching to the River Arno, just below the Ponte Vecchio.

Street numbering in Florence can be confusing until you realise that there are two systems: commercial premises have red numbers and residential premises have blue ones. In written addresses, the letter 'r' after a number stands for *rosso* (red); in other words, a commercial enterprise. In the centre of Florence there are far more commercial premises than residential, so bear in mind that Via Roma 7 (blue), for example, will be considerably further down the street than Via Roma 7r (red).

Opening Times

The museums of Florence are now open for more hours than ever before, with many of the major museums open all day, from early in the morning until the early evening. This flexibility means that you can often beat the queues by turning up during the siesta period, when many tourists, especially those in groups, take a break from sightseeing to have lunch; or in the late afternoon, just as many people are leaving. If you know exactly when you want to visit, you can also book tickets in advance for the Uffizi, Palazzo Vecchio, Bargello and Accademia by calling the Museum Reservation Line (tel: 055-294 883; open Mon–Fri 8.30am–6.30pm, Sat 8.30am–12.30pm). This is well worth doing, as it could potentially save you an hour's queuing per museum.

Smaller museums and most churches still close from 1pm to 4 or 5pm, as do all but a handful of shops. Monday is a bad day to visit Florence, since many museums, shops and restaurants are closed – we have attempted in this guide to recommend alternative things to do if you are here on a Monday. Bear in mind that ticket sales at museums stop 45 minutes before closing time. Museums also have a habit of closing rooms furthest from the exit well before the closing time, so late arrivers may not get to see the whole church or museum.

Left: symbolic statues in the Piazza della Signoria
Right: a plaster cast in the Galleria dell'Accademia

1. THE MAJOR LANDMARKS *(see maps, below & p23)*

This first day in Florence will be spent visiting the most famous monuments in the *centro storico* – the historic centre – including the Duomo (cathedral), the Battistero (Baptistry), the Piazza della Signoria and Palazzo Vecchio, the Uffizi gallery and the Ponte Vecchio. Suggestions are included for places to lunch along the way.

If your first day in Florence is a Sunday, Monday or Thursday, you will be able to do only the first part of this tour, as the Palazzo Vecchio closes at 2pm on Sunday and Thursday and the Uffizi Gallery is closed all day Monday. Alternative sights will be proposed at appropriate points.

Start in **Piazza del Duomo** (Cathedral Square). The best place for kick-starting yourself into the day with a strong black *espresso* is the **Sergio** bar, Piazza del Capitolo 1, on the south side of the square, which has seats outside offering good views of the majestic cathedral dome and Giotto's campanile. From here you can get a sense of the huge scale of the cathedral, once the largest church in Christendom, and still the fourth biggest in the world (after St Peter's in Rome, St Paul's in London and the cathedral in Milan).

Above: a view of the Duomo at night, from San Miniato

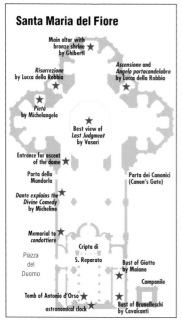

Santa Maria del Fiore

Main altar with bronze shrine by Ghiberti

Risurrezione by Lucca della Robbia

Ascensione and *Angelo portacandelabro* by Lucca della Robbia

Pietà by Michelangelo

Best view of *Last Judgment* by Vasari

Entrance for ascent of the dome

Porta della Mandorla

Porta dei Canonici (Canon's Gate)

Dante explains the Divine Comedy by Michelino

Memorial to condottiere

Cripta di S. Reparata

Piazza del Duomo

Bust of Giotto by Maiano

Campanile

Tomb of Antonio d'Orso

astronomical clock

Bust of Brunelleschi by Cavalcanti

The Duomo (the word comes from the Latin *Domus Dei*, House of God) was built as a place of worship but, just as importantly, it symbolises Florentine civic pride and the citizens' determination always to have the biggest and the best of everything. It took almost 150 years to build (from 1294 to 1436) and even then the neo-Gothic facade, the exuberance of which contrasts with the sober restraint of the buildings surrounding the square, was not added until the 19th century.

The Campanile and the Crypt

The bell tower, **Campanile di Giotto**, was designed by Giotto in 1331, six years before his death, and the cathedral's soaring central dome was built by Filippo Brunelleschi, the greatest architect and engineer of his day. As a tribute to Brunelleschi, no other building in Florence has been built as high as the dome since its completion in 1436, when the cathedral was consecrated by Pope Eugenius IV.

From Sergio's, you have to walk round to the front of the cathedral and join the fast-moving queue to get in (open Mon–Fri 10am–5pm, Thurs till 3.30pm, Sat till 4.45pm, Sun 1.30–4.45pm; admission free). Inside, the steps to the right lead down to the **crypt** (open Mon–Sat 10am–5pm; entrance fee). Here you will find Brunelleschi's simple grave. The inscription on the tomb slab compares him to Icarus, the mythical hero who learned to fly but then plunged to his death when he flew too close to the sun and it melted his wings. Brunelleschi's is the only tomb in the cathedral (although there are various memorials); his burial within its walls was a singular honour granted in recognition of his genius in building the dome. The rest of the crypt contains the ruins of **Santa Reparata**, the original church on the site.

Turn left out of the crypt and right along the north wall of the cathedral. You will pass a fresco of **Sir John Hawkwood** on horseback, painted by Paolo Uccello in 1436. Hawkwood was an English *condottiere* (mercenary), whose hired soldiers often fought for Florence. Other cities honoured military heroes with equestrian statues in stone or bronze; the fact that Hawkwood was commemorated only in a fresco is often cited as an example of Florentine miserliness.

Right: daily life goes on outside the Duomo

Nearby you will also see a painting of Dante outside the walls of Florence, symbolising his exile; the picture was commissioned in 1465 to commemorate the bicentenary of the poet's birth.

Ahead lies the sanctuary, with its lovely stained-glass windows (mainly 15th-century in date). Soaring high above is the newly restored fresco of the *Last Judgement* that Vasari painted in 1572–79 on the underside of the enormous dome. Critics have questioned whether the quality of Vasari's work justified the US$6 million that was spent on their restoration. Vasari intended these scenes to rival the work of Michelangelo in the Sistine Chapel in Rome,

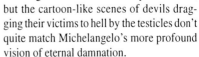

but the cartoon-like scenes of devils dragging their victims to hell by the testicles don't quite match Michelangelo's more profound vision of eternal damnation.

If you want to take a closer look at these vast figures, you can climb up to the dome. To do so, exit the cathedral and circle round to the left to the little door in the southern flank of the building signposted **Cupola del Duomo** (open Mon–Fri 8.30am–7pm, Sat 8.30am–5.40pm; entrance fee). You need stamina to climb the 464 spiralling stairs to the top of the dome, but you will be rewarded by intimate glimpses of the dome's construction on the way up, and a fabulous view of the city once you reach the top. Climbers descending the stairs frequently pass encouraging remarks to those still arduously toiling upwards. Before Brunelleschi, nobody had built such a massive dome since Roman times; he visited Rome to study the 2nd-century AD Pantheon in order to reinvent the ancient technique of building upwards in decreasing circles of interlocking brick.

The Baptistry

If you have gone to the top of the dome, you will probably not have the energy to climb the 285 steps of the **Campanile di Giotto**, on the right as you leave the cathedral (open Mon–Fri 6.30am–7pm, Sat 8.30am–5.40pm; entrance fee). Save this for another day, perhaps, and walk over to the little octagonal **Battistero** (Baptistry) to the west of the cathedral. This has limited opening hours (Mon–Sat noon–7pm, Sun 8.30am–2pm; entrance fee) but no matter – it is the exterior that is really important.

Florentines have always exaggerated the antiquity of the Baptistry. Evidence suggests that it was built in the 6th or 7th century using Roman masonry. In the 12th century it was taken under the wing of the Calimala, the guild of wool importers, who paid for its marble cladding of green geometric

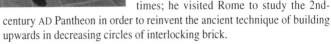

Top right: stained glass in the Duomo. **Left:** carriage rides from the Baptistry
Right: striking mosaics decorate the Baptistry ceiling

designs on a white background, an innovative design admired and imitated elsewhere in Tuscany (the Duomo of Florence follows its example). Set into this 10th-century building, one of the oldest in Florence, are three sets of bronze doors. Those to the south were made in the 1330s by the Pisan artist Andrea Pisano and illustrate the *Life of St John the Baptist*, patron saint of Florence. Although they are early works, they exhibit Renaissance characteristics – dynamism in the dramatic grouping of figures, fluency and immediacy, all in contrast to the static spirituality of the Gothic art of the 13th and 14th centuries. Pisano was several decades ahead of his time.

The Renaissance proper is conventionally dated to 1401 when a competition was held to select an artist for the remaining doors *(see History and Culture, page 11)*. The winner, Lorenzo Ghiberti (1378–1455), first made the doors that fill the north entrance, illustrating New Testament scenes, completed in 1424. He then made the superb **Porta del Paradiso** (Gates of Paradise), the east entrance facing the cathedral, so called because Michelangelo hailed these doors as suitable for the entrance to paradise. What you see now are casts of the original panels, illustrating Old Testament scenes (the originals, completed in 1452, are displayed in the Museo dell'Opera del Duomo – *see page 46)*. The door frames, however, are original and contain portrait busts of 24 leading Renaissance artists – Ghiberti himself is the bald-headed figure, third up from the bottom in the centre of the doors. If you do go inside the Baptistry, you will find a ceiling covered in striking mosaics that depict the main events of the Old and New Testaments, from the story of Creation to the Last Judgement. Executed in sparkling gold, ruby and turquoise glass cubes, they are the work of various 13th-century artists. Beneath the dome are the remains of the pavement of 1209, inlaid with the signs of the Zodiac. Two Roman columns have been incorporated into the graceful marble cladding of the walls to the right of the altar, where they flank the beautiful marble tomb of Pope John XXIII, with a bronze effigy of the sleeping pope by Donatello (1425). The Pope died on a visit to Florence in 1419.

When you have seen enough, walk down the south flank of the cathedral, to the east end, and turn right down Via del Proconsolo. On the left you will pass No 12, the **Palazzo Nonfinito** (Unfinished Palace), begun by

Bountalenti in 1593 and never completed; it contains the **Museo di Antropologia** (Anthropology Museum; open daily except Tues and Sun 9am–12.30pm; entrance fee). If you have the time, it is well worth dipping into this huge and fascinating museum, which has 35 rooms full of relics from all the remote, unusual and fascinating corners of the globe that have captured the attention of anthropologists over the past 150 years.

There are interesting relics collected by Captain James Cook before he met his death in Hawaii in 1779 on his final voyage to the Pacific, and there are display cases packed with masks, drums, musical instruments, bows, arrows and snares, objects designed for war and ritual, theatre and magic, music and celebration from every continent of the globe.

Turning left out of the museum, take the first right, Via del Corso, passing the **Banca Toscana** on the right – the exchange rate here is good and the banking hall features a fresco of the Virgin, St John and St Zenobius.

To the Piazza della Signoria

Opposite the bank, go through a tunnel into Via Santa Margherita. On the left is the little church of **Santa Marherita** (open Mon–Sat 10am–2pm, 3–4.30pm, Sun 10.30–11.30am; admission free), built in 1200, where Dante often caught sight of Beatrice Portinare, the daughter of a wealthy banker, whom he was to idealise in his poetry. Beatrice was always chaperoned by her nurse, Monna Tessa, as depicted in the painting (1991) by Mario d'Elia on the left-hand wall of the nave. The painting on the opposite side shows the *Marriage of Beatrice Portinari* (1928) by R. Sarb, but the marriage was not to Dante. Although he became obsessed with 'the glorious Lady of my mind', Beatrice was married at the age of 17 to Simone de' Bardi, son of another wealthy banker, but she died only seven years later, in 1291.

Both Beatrice, and her nurse (who died in 1327) are buried on the left-hand side of the nave, in the Portinari family vault, where the 14th-centry tomb

Above: visitors gather outside the Loggia dei Lanzi

slab carved with the figure of an elderly woman, is always marked by a bunch of fresh flowers. The church is often used for baroque chamber music and organ recitals – see the notice at the entrance.

At the end of the street, on the right, is the **Casa di Dante** (open Mon–Sat 10am–6pm, Sun 10am–2pm; entrance fee). This much-restored medieval house, with a truncated 13th-century tower, is claimed as Dante's birthplace and contains a small museum on his life and work – the downstairs rooms (entrance free) are used for exhibitions of contemporary art.

Turn right in Via Dante Alighieri and head straight on, until you come to Via de'Calzaiuoli (passing the renowned ice-cream shop, Pèrche No!, on the left at Via dei Tavolini 19r). Opposite is the church of **Orsanmichele**, which was once a grain store (open daily 9am–noon, 4–6pm; currently under renovation; admission free). Walk round the church, to the right, and down Via dei Tavolini where you can study the statues in the wall niches. Each of these niches belonged to one of the city's powerful guilds, who commissioned artists to portray their patron saints. The most famous statue, Donatello's *St George*, is now replaced by a copy; the original can be seen in the Bargello Museum *(see page 45)*.

At the back, an aerial corridor links Orsanmichele to the 13th-century **Palazzo del'Arte della Lana** (Wool Guild Palace). The entrance to the church is

below. The centrepiece of this astonishingly rich Gothic church is Andrea Orcagna's elaborate tabernacle (1459), decorated with scenes from the *Life of the Virgin*, enclosing Bernardo Daddi's painting of the *Madonna* (1347). Turn left out of the church, left again in Via dei Lamberti, passing Donatello's statue of *St Mark* in the first niche, then right in Via dei Calzaiuoli, to **Piazza della Signoria**.

This fine, spacious square is now traffic-free. Towering over everything is the battlemented facade and campanile of the Palazzo Vecchio, which was built as the seat of city government between 1299 and 1322. This dwarfs even the huge heroic figure of *David* (a copy – Michelangelo's original is in the Accademia, *see page 32*), Bandinelli's rather lumpy figure of *Hercules* (1534) and the licentious nymphs of Ammanati's *Neptune Fountain* (1575). These works of art, all fronting the palace, symbolise Florence in various ways – for example, David as a figure of defiance against tyranny, Hercules as the mythical founder of the city and Neptune as a metaphor for the city's naval fleet, created by Cosimo I. To the right, sheltering under the **Loggia dei Lanzi** (named after Cosimo I's bodyguard, the lancers), are several antique statues, Cellini's *Perseus* grasping the severed head of Medusa, and Giambologna's renowned *Rape of the Sabine Women* (1583).

Above: the Palazzo Vecchio
Right: Giambologna's *Rape of the Sabine Women*

If you are ready for lunch, the **Pizzeria Il David** is the best bargain in the square. Or seek out tiny **Pasquini**, tucked away in Via Val di Limona, a narrow street behind the Mercato Nuovo, for a simple lunch of pasta or, the more substantial roast suckling pig. For an authentic Florentine lunch, go to the tripe stand alongside the market place (to the left of the bronze boar) for a stand-up *lampredotto* sandwich (pigs' intestines) or a dish of *trippa alla Fiorentin*. Alternatively, the classy **Rivoire**, right on the square, offers ice-cream and pastries with views of the historic buildings (closed Monday).

Your choice will partly depend on the day of the week – as will your next move. The afternoon will be spent visiting the Palazzo Vecchio and the Uffizi but not if it is a Sunday, when the Palazzo Vecchio is closed in the afternoon: instead you might like to visit the Bargello *(page 45)* or spend longer in the Uffizi. Another option is to walk off lunch by heading for San Miniato *(see page 52)* – always popular with the Florentines on a Sunday. If it is Monday, you can visit the Palazzo Vecchio, but not the Uffizi; instead, try the Museo dell'Opera del Duomo *(see page 48)*.

The Palazzo Vecchio

After lunch cross the Piazza della Signoria again, negotiating the crowds, pigeons and horse-drawn carriages. Passing *David*, climb the steps of the **Palazzo Vecchio** to enter a *cortile* (courtyard), designed in 1453 by Michelangelo, that features charming *putti* and a dolphin fountain – Vasari's copy of one made by Verrocchio in 1470. The courtyard's frescoes, also by Vasari, depict Austrian cities and were painted to make Joanna of Austria feel at home on the occasion of her marriage to Francesco de'Medici in 1565.

Beyond the courtyard is the ticket office for the **Quartieri Monumentali** (open in summer, Tues, Wed and Sat 9am–7pm, Mon and Fri to 11pm,

Sun and Thur to 2pm; no late opening in winter; entrance fee). If you have children, you may want to enquire here (or tel: 055-276 8244) about the **Museo di Ragazzi**, an organisation that runs workshops for children and tours of secret passageways and other parts of the palace not normally open to the public (advance reservation required). The magnificent state apartments on the first floor, starting with the vast Salone dei Cinquecento, were used for meetings of the Florentine Grand Council under the reign of Savonarola, the religious despot who regarded artists as heretics. It was later transformed by Giorgio Vasari whose frescoes depict the military victories of Duke Cosimo I. Statues of wrestling figures, by Michelangelo, Vincenzo de'Rossi and Giambologna line the walls. Off the Salone dei Cinque-

Left: the dolphin fountain in the courtyard of the Palazzo Vecchio

city itineraries

cento is the study of Francesco de'Medici (*Lo Studiolo*; 1575), a suitable retreat for the reclusive prince whose parents, Duke Cosimo I and Eleonora di Toledo, are depicted on the walls. Beyond lies a suite of rooms, all frescoed by Vasari and used by the Medici popes, one-time rulers of Florence; several offer fine views over the city. The rooms of Eleonora di Toledo, with feminine virtue depicted on the ceiling frescoes, are especially lovely.

Next is the most splendid chamber, the **Sala dei Gigli**, with walls covered in the gold fleur-de-lys symbol of Florence. Here, there is a marble statue of St John the Baptist (patron saint of Florence) as a boy, and Donatello's *Judith and Holofernes* (1460), originally placed in the Piazza della Signoria after the expulsion of the Medici in 1494 – the virtuous Judith slaying the tyrant Holofernes symbolises Florentine triumph over despotism. Off the Sala dei Gigli is the **Cancelleria**, with a painting and bust of Niccolò Machiavelli who used the room as an office when he was chancellor.

The Uffizi Gallery

Steps now lead down and out of the Palazzo Vecchio, and if you exit past the ticket office, you will find yourself looking up the long narrow courtyard that lies between the two wings of the **Galleria degli Uffizi** (open Tues–Sun 8.15am–6.50pm; ticket office closes at 6.05pm; entrance fee). The courtyard will be thronging with people. Living statues pose as Galileo or Michelangelo and perform a mime act if you make a donation; buskers entertain on guitar and lute; street hawkers display their posters, leather goods, sunglasses and African sculptures; portrait artists will draw your likeness. Unless you have had the foresight to book tickets in advance *(see page 21),* you will have to walk to the far side of the courtyard, to the Arno embankment, and join the queue for entry.

Your patience will be rewarded by a close encounter with some of the world's best-known works of art. The Uffizi is unique in that most of its paintings were created in Florence, by Florentine artists, for Florentine patrons.

Above: amateur artists set up their easels outside the Uffizi Gallery

Many were commissioned, collected or inherited by the Medici, whose last surviving family member, Anna Maria Ludovica, bequeathed the entire collection to the citizens of Florence at her death in 1743. That extraordinary and selfless act was respected by her successors, and so the city is blessed with a collection that is far more coherent than many, allowing visitors to see how Renaissance art developed during the 15th and 16th centuries.

The Uffizi itself was built by Vasari in 1560 to provide offices (*uffici* in Italian) for the Medici administration. The building has always been used by the Medici to display prize works of art from their collections – including numerous antique Roman and Greek statues lining the corridor that runs in a U-shape around the three wings of the Uffizi.

The gallery's collection begins with Tuscan masterpieces from the pre-Renaissance era. Cimabue is credited by Vasari with reintroducing the art of painting to Italy by learning from Greek artists, and his late-12th century *Maestà* (or *Virgin Enthroned*) clearly owes a debt to Byzantine art in the formal composition of the subject, and the stylisation of faces and drapery. Giotto learned from Cimabue and introduced the greater degree of naturalness to painting that can be seen in his *Ognissanti Madonna* (1310).

Anticipating the Renaissance

It is not easy to pinpoint the precise moment when Gothic art gave way to the Renaissance. Simone Martini's *Annunciation* (1333) in Room 3 seems to anticipate the Renaissance artist's desire to create a realistic sense of space, though chronologically it is firmly in the Gothic era. By contrast, Masaccio's *Madonna and Child with St Anne* (1424) in Room 7 is clearly within the Gothic idiom of religious painting, with little angels surrounding the Virgin, just like those in Giotto's work. But Masaccio was one of the pioneers of the Renaissance and there is something subtly different about the central grouping of the three figures in this work – they are almost sculptural in their three-dimensional depth, and more like living, breathing humans than those in any of the earlier paintings.

Several other works in Room 7 represent early Renaissance artists exploring purely secular subjects – for the first time in Western art since antiquity. Uccello's *Battle of San Remo* (1456) celebrates the Florentine victory over their long-time rivals, the Sienese. Piero della Francesca's portraits (1465)

city itineraries

are unflinching in their warts-and-all portrayal of the *Duke Federico da Montefeltro* and his far-from beautiful wife, *Battista Sforza*.

By the time we get to Room 10, with its glowing and ethereal Botticelli paintings of *Primavera* (1478) and the *Birth of Venus* (1485) we are firmly in the Renaissance world, and its fascination with pagan and Platonic symbolism. Botticelli is hardly typical – in some ways his style and subject matter are unique, and even he went back to purely Christian religious painting later in life, under the influence of the teachings of Savonarola, as you can see from his gorgeous *Madonna of the Magnificat*. But Botticelli did help open the door for other painters to choose characters and stories from classical mythology, and from then on artists and their patrons had the choice between the Virgin – as in Leonardo's *Adoration of the Magi* (1482) in Room 15, or Michelangelo's *Holy Family Tondo* (1504) in Room 25 – or Venus, as in Titian's profoundly seductive *Venus of Urbino* (1538), Room 28.

Most of the Uffizi's 45 rooms contains at least one masterpiece, and the artists represented read like a roll-call of the greatest painters of all time: Dürer and Caravaggio, Bellini and Giorgioni, Hans Holbein and Hans Memling, Raphael, Rubens and Rembrandt. There are also magnificent views from the windows overlooking the Arno, and from the café at the other end, whose tables overlook the Piazza della Signoria.

Once you have seen enough, leave the Uffizi, walk down to the Arno and turn right to the **Ponte Vecchio** (Old Bridge). Wander with the crowds, enjoying the views from the bridge and the bustle of traders. However, this is the heart of tourist land, so a good restaurant is hard to find. For a glass of wine and a nibble, go to the tiny, friendly wine bar, **Le Volpi e L'Uva**, behind Piazza Santa Felicità (closes at 8pm). Try **Celestino** (tel: 055 2396574) in the piazza itself or, for something more authentic, go a little further afield. The inventive fare in the **Osteria Santo Spirito** (in the piazza of the same name, tel: 055 2382383) attracts a young crowd, and **Angiolino**, in Via Santo Spirito (tel: 055 2398976), does traditional Tuscan food in a rustic atmosphere. For a chic choice, go to **Beccofino**, on the river *(see Eating and Drinking page 77).*

Left: Michelangelo's *Holy Family*
Above: Botticelli's *Birth of Venus*

2. MICHELANGELO
AND THE MEDICI *(see map, p33)*

Today you will hit the Michelangelo trail, visiting some of his best works and unravelling his somewhat ambivalent relationship with the Medici family; in between you will visit the markets around San Lorenzo and some very upmarket shops in the Santa Maria Novella district.

Head as early as possible for the **Galleria dell'Accademia**, Via Ricasoli 58 (open Tues–Sun 8.15am–6.50pm; entrance fee) because this gallery attracts a huge number of visitors and long queues build up, especially at Easter and in the peak summer months. If you find a queue has already formed, don't despair – it moves quite quickly (if you've time for a coffee first, try the typical neighbourhood bar on the corner of Via Ricasoli and Via degli Alfani, just south of the entrance).

The queues can be explained in two words: Michelangelo's *David* (1504) – the original statue, as opposed to the copy that now stands in front of the Palazzo Vecchio. Its current setting is far from satisfactory – it was moved here in 1873 as a precaution against weathering and pigeon droppings – but the towering figure still exerts a magnetic force on visitors. *David* is both a celebration of the adolescent male body and a symbol of Florentine aspiration – her citizens liked to think of themselves as brave combatants, ready to fight any tyrannical Goliath who threatened their liberty (be it the Pope, the Medici, the Holy Roman Emperor or neighbouring city states).

Michelangelo shared these republican instincts. He offered to carve *Samson Overcoming a Philistine* to symbolise the new republic after Piero de'Medici fled the city in 1494. He never fulfilled his promise because he was too busy doing other things – fulfilling commissions, in fact, for those same enemies of the republic, the Medici popes. Part of the enigma of Michelangelo is the fact that he fought against the Medici

Above: admiring exhibits in the Galleria dell'Accademia
Left: Michelangelo's *David*

but depended on their patronage. On display here is the unfinished *Quattro Prigioni* (*Four Slaves*), originally intended for the tomb of Pope Julius II.

His work is the highlight of the Accademia, but there are others of interest – do not miss the excellent plaster models by Lorenzo Burtolini (1797–1850) displayed in the **Salone delle Toscane**. These preliminary working models were copied in sculpted marble to produce the final work of art.

From Piazza San Marco to the Cappella dei Magi

From the Accademia, turn right and head for the **Piazza San Marco**. In term time you will weave your way through chatting groups of art students who study at the Accademia, which was founded in 1563 by Vasari, with Michelangelo as one of its members. You will also pass, directly opposite the gallery exit, the Libreria LEF bookshop (Via Ricasoli 105–7/r); here you will find a comprehensive stock of art books, postcards and posters.

Straight ahead, in Piazza San Marco, is the **Museo di San Marco** (Mon–Fri 8.15am–1.50pm, Sat till 6.50pm, Sun till 7pm, closed the first, third and fifth Sunday and second and fourth Monday of each month; entrance fee), housed in a group of conventual buildings. Many famous names are connected with San Marco. Cosimo de' Medici paid for the building of this monastery, which was occupied by Dominican friars from the nearby hill town of Fiesole in 1436. Fra Angelico spent most of his life within its walls and the museum contains most of his paintings, as well as some superb frescoes: his *Crucifixion* (1442) is in the Chapter House, his *Annunciation* is at the top of the staircase leading to the dormitory, and a series of almost abstract pictures, intended as aids to religious contemplation, are in cells 1 to 10 of the dormitory (other artists were involved in the remaining cell paintings). Savonarola was made prior of the convent in 1491 and his cells (Nos 12 to 14) contain various mementoes.

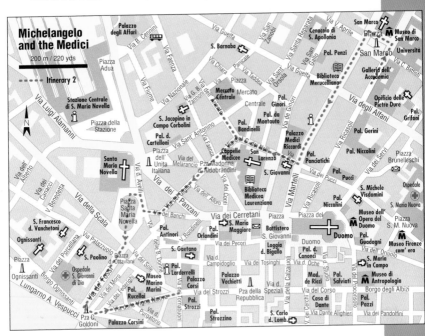

Emerging from San Marco, turn right and walk to the western end of the square and look right, up Via Cavour. The big palace with barred windows, ornamented with rams' heads, stands on the site of the garden in which Cosimo de' Medici displayed his collection of antique sculptures and where, in the school of art, the young Michelangelo studied drawing. There is a garden centre and florist's shop in what remains of the garden.

Now head in the opposite direction down Via Cavour to reach the **Palazzo Medici-Riccardi**, on the right. This somewhat grim (and deliberately unostentatious) palace was built for Cosimo de' Medici between 1444 and 1464. It was from here that Cosimo and his heirs operated as unofficial rulers of Florence until Piero fled the city in 1494. The courtyard walls are studded with antique inscriptions, and the renovated **Cappella dei Magi** (open Thur–Tues 9am–7pm; entrance fee) is home to the stunningly colourful fresco of Benozzo Gozzoli's *Journey of the Magi* (1459), in which members of the Medici family are depicted among the royal retinue.

Leaving the palace, turn right and right again, in Via de' Gori, and you will plunge into the midst of the huge and bustling San Lorenzo street market. There will be time to explore this later – now, the aim is to see the Laurentian Library before it closes. As you weave through the stalls you will see an equestrian statue of *Giovanni delle Bande Nere*, the warrior father of Duke Cosimo I, by Bandinelli (1540).

The Medici Library and the Mercato Centrale

To the left of the statue is the bare, unfinished facade of San Lorenzo (to which we shall return); to the left of the church is the entrance to the **Biblioteca Medicea Laurenziana** (open daily 8.30am–1.30pm; entrance fee), which lies at the far end of a serene cloister, from where there are unusual views of Giotto's campanile and the cathedral dome. The library, with its extraordinary vestibule and staircase, was designed by Michelangelo from 1524. His client was the Medici pope, Clement VII, and the library was built to house part of the famous collection of antique Greek and Latin manuscripts collected by Cosimo and Lorenzo de' Medici. Depending on what's currently on display you may see Pliny the Younger's hand-written text, a 1436 printing of Plutarch's *Moralia* (Morals) and a Greek edition (1496) of the works of the 15th-century humanist, Poliziano, with handwritten notations.

Once you have seen the library, it may be time to consider lunch. Leaving the quiet cloister, plunge back into the mêlée of Florentine street life. Surrounding the San Lorenzo market, there is a good choice of *trattorias*, many of which feed the market workers at lunchtime. Hidden behind the stalls at Via della Ruosina 2r is **Da Mario**, a simple family-run business where the

Above: resting in the Palazzo Medici-Riccardi courtyard
Right: mushrooms for sale in the Mercato Centrale

Florentine *zuppe* are tasty and wholesome (open Mon–Sat for lunch only). Alternatively, the **Casa del Vino** at Via dell' Ariento 16r serves delicious snacks and a good choice of wines by the glass. The popular **Trattoria Za-Za**, at the back of the market *(see Eating and Drinking, page 83)*, has a decent set-price menu. There are also plenty of fast-food and 'pizza by the slice' joints. If you are on a budget, you can snack in the Central Market – in which case, turn right out of the Medici Chapel, then left in Via dell'Ariento, passing through San Lorenzo market. The stalls next to the church are geared to tourists and sell T-shirts, leatherwork and souvenirs. The deeper in you go, the more stalls you will find catering to the needs of ordinary Florentines, selling bargain-priced clothes, shoes, fabrics and table linen.

In 1990 the city administration tried to close down the market – at least, that part of it that crowds around the church. Eventually the police gave up in the face of determined resistance from stallholders. As you walk through the market, don't neglect the little shops either side of the street, almost hidden by the stalls, where you will find all sorts of necessities for sale.

Halfway up, on the right, is the entrance to the huge **Mercato Centrale** (Central Market). The stalls on the ground floor sell an abundance of meat, fish and cheese, while upstairs, under the towering glass and cast-iron roof, you can buy fruit, vegetables and flowers – and you will not find better quality or keener prices than here. Also upstairs is a delightful bar where you can enjoy a coffee or drink immersed in the animated buzz of conversation of shoppers and stallholders. You can also sample some Florentine specialities sold from the cooked-meat stalls or cafés downstairs – the *porchetta* (roast suckling pig) is delicious.

San Lorenzo

After lunch, it is time to explore **San Lorenzo** church (open Mon–Sat 7am–5pm; entrance fee), which is entered through a door in the unfinished facade. The interior was mainly designed by Brunelleschi and is remarkable for the elegant sobriety of the grey and white walls. Just before the central domed crossing are two huge marble pulpits carved by Donatello with scenes from the *Passion* and *Resurrection of Christ*.

To the north of the pulpits, Bronzino's huge fresco of the Martyrdom of St Lawrence (1569), is unmissable. To the left, and often overlooked, is a more recent painting by Pietro Annigoni (1910–88) of the young Jesus with Joseph in a carpenter's workshop.

The church was once used for state funerals, and early members of the Medici family are buried here. Cosimo, who died in 1474, is buried in a vault in front of the high altar. His father, Giovanni di Bicci de' Medici (died 1429), the wealthy banker who founded the powerful dynasty, is buried in the **Sagrestia Vecchia** (Old Sacristy), off the north transept, built by Brunelleschi as the family mausoleum. Donatello made the bronze entrance doors (1437–43) with their animated figures of apostles, saints, martyrs and fathers of the Church. The circular *tondi* in the chapel walls depicting the Evangelists and the Life of St John the Evangelist in terracotta and plaster relief are his, too (1435–43).

Giovanni's sarcophagus in the centre of the chapel is by Buggiani (1434); his grandsons, Giovanni (died 1463) and Piero de' Medici (died 1469), are buried in the huge urn-like sarcophagi of porphyry and bronze set into the walls and designed by Verrocchio (1472).

Later members of the Medici family are buried in the **Sagrestia Nuova** (New Sacristy), which was the last – and perhaps the greatest – of all Michelangelo's works for his aristocratic patrons in Florence. This is situated off the opposite transept and now has a separate entrance, which involves leaving the church and walking round the southern side to the eastern end, where you will find the entrance to the **Cappelle Medicee** (Medici Chapels) on Piazza Madonna degli Aldobrandini (daily 8.15am–5pm, closed first, third and fifth Monday and second and fourth Sunday of the month; entrance fee). When you enter you will first pass through the extraordinary **Cappella dei Principi** (Chapel of the Princes), the walls of which are covered in costly, multi-coloured marble; the enormous sarcophagi commemorate the 16th- and 17th-century Grand Dukes of Tuscany.

From here, a corridor leads on to the Sagrestia Nuova; although sober in contrast to the Cappelle Medicee, it contains some stupendous sculptures. The modest tomb of Lorenzo de'Medici is marked by Michelangelo's unfinished *Madonna and Child*. To the left is the tomb of Lorenzo's grand-

son, also called Lorenzo (1492–1519), draped with the figures of Dawn and Dusk, while opposite is the tomb of Lorenzo's son, Giuliano, with the awesome figures of *Night* and *Day*, symbolising the temporal and eternal forces of nature, and carved between 1520 and 1533. Ironically, while working on them, Michelangelo was involved in the battle against the besieging forces of the Medici, to keep Florence an independent republic. When that battle was lost it is thought that Michelangelo hid from his patrons in this chapel. On the walls of a small room are the charcoal sketches he made at this time.

Santa Maria Novella

Next, head along Via del Giglio to **Piazza Santa Maria Novella** and the **church** (open Mon, Thur and Sat 9.30am–5pm, Fri and Sun 1.30–5pm; entrance fee). There is enough to see here to fill an hour or so. The vast square was originally used for chariot races, which explains the granite obelisks at each end of the green, resting on the backs of Giambologna's tortoises (1608), which marked the turning points on the track. The church has a graceful facade of green-and-white marble, incorporating the name of the Rucellai family and their symbol – a billowing ship's sail, representing trade. The family, who paid the architect Alberti to build the facade in 1470, formed a marriage alliance with the Medici – you will see that family's ring-and-ostrich-feather symbol among the complex geometric patterning.

Santa Maria Novella is entered through the cemetery to the right. The wall arcade surrounding the cypress-shaded grounds is carved with the coats-of-arms of the bankers, merchants and clothiers whose family members are buried here. Built in the 14th-century, the cemetery is a reminder that the city was then in the grips of the Black Death. Boccaccio used the setting of this church as the springboard for his rambling *Decameron*, in which a group of aristocrats escape to a villa outside Florence to avoid the disease. To entertain each other, they take turns to tell the 100 tales referred to in the title.

The interior of the church is a breathtaking masterpiece of Gothic design, the soaring arches of the nave emphasised with alternating bands of white and grey stone. Hanging in the nave is Giotto's huge, emblematic *Crucifix* (1290).

Another Crucifixion features in Masaccio's fresco the *Trinity, Mary and St John* (1427), in the north aisle, a landmark in the development of perspective in early Renaissance art. Behind the

Left: the cloister of San Lorenzo. **Above:** Santa Maria Novella. **Right:** one of Giambologna's tortoises

high altar are Ghirlandaio's colourful frescoes, the *Life of the Virgin* and *St John the Baptist* (1485–90). These repay detailed study and give a good idea of the living conditions of wealthy Florentines in the late 15th century. Equally compelling are Filippino Lippi's frescoes in the Strozzi Chapel, to the right of the altar (1497–1502). Lippi's theatrical style and love of the bizarre are well displayed in these scenes from the *Lives of St Philip and St John the Evangelist* (1502), which form the monumental setting for Benedetto da Maiano's tomb (1486) for the wealthy banker Filippo Strozzi.

There are more notable frescoes in the **Chiostro Verde** (Green Cloister), including Uccello's dramatic *Noah and the Flood* (1450), but you may have to see them another time, due to the restrictive opening times (Mon–Sat 9am–2pm, Sun 8am–1pm; entrance fee). The cloister was so named for the predominant colour of Ucello's frescoes. Damaged by the floods of 1966, they have been leached of much of their colour, but they still remain powerful and surprisingly modern in concept: Noah's Ark is not the traditional stumpy boat, but a vast, futuristic ship. Ucello painted an equally dramatic representation of the Flood, with fish swimming among drowned babies, and people clinging to branches and the remaining pieces of dry land.

Fine Shopping

For now, head left across the square, into Piazza degli Ottaviani and Via de' Fossi. The latter has a number of good shops to browse around. **Neri** (57r) sells antiques and **G. Lisio** (41r) has superb handwoven textiles and tapestries. At **Antonio Frilli** (26r) you can buy (expensive) reproductions of Florence's most famous statues. At the bottom of the street, leading to Piazza C Goldoni, there are more interesting shops worth investigating: in Borgo Ognissanti, to the right, they include the BM English-language bookshop (4r) and **Galleria Faustina** (23r), which sells modern Italian paintings and lithographs. If you are more interested in high fashion than high art, turn left to Via della Vigna Nuova and Via de' Tornabuoni, both of which are lined with chic boutiques and shops selling haute couture.

If you don't spend too much, you may want to reward yourself with dinner in the elegant **Cantinetta Antinori**, at the top of Via de' Tornabuoni *(see Eating Out)*. Alternatively try **Trattoria Garga** (Via del Moro 48r, tel: 2398898, closed Mon). The decor is ecentric but the atmosphere is lively and the food highly creative. Budget travellers may prefer to make their way to **Capocaccia** (Lungarno Corsini 12r), near Ponte Santa Trínita, a wine bar serving generous salads and sandwiches and is the perfect spot from which to watch the sun setting over the Arno.

Above: fragment of a colourful fresco in Santa Maria Novella

city itineraries

3. OLTRARNO: PITTI PALACE AND BOBOLI GARDENS *(see map, p40)*

Today's itinerary heads south to Oltrarno – literally 'beyond the Arno' – to visit the Pitti Palace, with its five museums, the Boboli Gardens for outstanding views, and the Brancacci Chapel.

Cross the river by the **Ponte Vecchio** (literally 'Old Bridge'), built in its present form in 1345 and the only one in the city that did not get blown up in August 1944 by retreating Nazis (the others have since been reconstructed). As you cross the bridge, note the corridor on the left-hand side, high above the jewellers' shops, which is known as the **Corridoio Vasariano** (Vasari's Corridor), after its designer (for visiting times, enquire in person at the information desk at the Uffizi). It links the Palazzo Vecchio, seat of the Tuscan administration, with the Palazzo Pitti, home of the Medici Grand Dukes from 1550. The rulers of Florence and Tuscany could walk along this corridor without having to mingle with the common herd. On the opposite side of the river, as you walk down Via de' Guicciardini, you will see the corridor again in front of **Santa Felicità** church, on the left.

Have a look inside this church, which has two remarkable works by the Mannerist artist, Pontormo, an *Annunciation* and a *Deposition* (both of 1525–28). Mary McCarthy (in *The Stones of Florence*) pro-

Above: the grand facade of the Pitti Palace
Right: the opulent interior is breathtaking

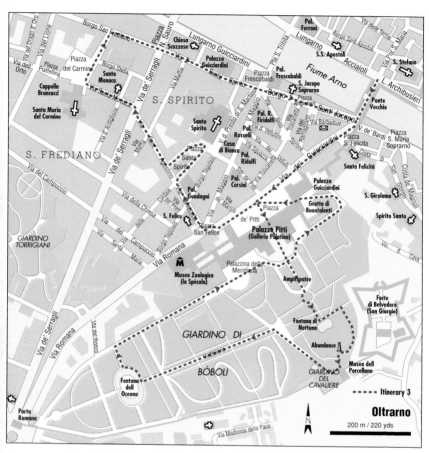

fessed to find these works decadent, but she accurately described their extraordinary colours – peppermint pink, orchid, gold-apricot, pomegranate and iridescent salmon. Turning left out of the church, walk down to the Piazza de'Pitti where, opposite the palace, you can have a drink at the charming pavement bar simply called Il Caffe.

The Pitti Palace

The **Palazzo Pitti** (Pitti Palace) was begun in the late 1450s for the banker Luca Pitti, but the cost of the building brought him to the verge of bankruptcy and his heirs sold it to Eleonora di Toledo, the Spanish-born wife of Duke Cosimo I, in 1549. The Medici moved here in 1550 and from then onwards it served as the home of Tuscany's rulers, gradually being expanded to its present immense bulk. We shall spend the morning in the **Galleria Palatina**, which contains outstanding works of art (open Tues–Sat 8.30am–6.50pm, Sun 8.30am–1.50pm; entrance fee).

Before the so-called Royal Apartments, there is a series of sumptuous antechambers containing some notable paintings and other objects. Filippo Lippi's beautiful *tondo* of the *Madonna and Child* and Rubens' *Three Graces*

city itineraries

hang in the Sala di Prometeo. The Sala di Bagni, decorated with stucco nymphs and four marble Nereides, was designed as part of a suite of apartments for the Emperor Napoleon after he had conquered northern Italy.

Move on to the five former reception rooms decorated with Pietro da Cortona's rich frescoes. The hunting scenes in the Sala di Saturno (Saturn Room) were never completed, but here hangs Raphael's tender *Madonna della Seggiola (circa* 1515). The Sala di Giove (Jupiter room, formerly the throne room) contains Andrea del Sarto's rather effeminate *St John the Baptist* and another Raphael, the serene and virtuosic *Donna Valeta*, said to be a portrait of Lucrezia delle Rovere. Fra Bartolomeo's recently restored and astounding *Pietà* is also here. The ceiling in the Sala di Marte (Mars Room) is covered with graphic battle scenes, but the room is dominated by Reubens' vast canvas, the *Consequences of War* (1638).

The Sala di Apollo contains several Titians, including the mysterious *Portrait of a Grey-eyed Gentleman* and a delightful *Maddalena*. In the centre of the last room, the Sala di Venere (Venus Room), a fine marble *Venus* by Canova emerges from her bath. Look out also for Titian's portrait, known as *La Bella*; the model featured may well be the same one who posed for his *Venus of Urbino*, which is now in the Uffizi.

After your visit to the Palatine Gallery, you may like to relax over coffee and cakes in the café on the south-eastern corner of the courtyard. There is also a good bookshop to explore on the opposite corner. It specialises in volumes on art history and also sells Florentine handicrafts – including convincing reproductions of Renaissance jewellery, bronzes, paintings, porcelain and engraved glass.

In addition to the Palatine Gallery there are five other museums to explore within the Pitti Palace complex, all of a specialist nature. They are the **Grand Ducal Treasures Museum** (Museo degli Argenti), the **Gallery of Modern Art** (Museo del Arte Moderna – for which read late-19th century to the immediate post-war period), the **Costume Gallery** and the **Carriage Museum** (all open Tues–Sun 8.30am–1.50pm).

Boboli Gardens

Admission to the **Porcelain Museum** (*see page 42*) is included in the price of admission to the **Boboli Gardens** (open daily 9am to dusk, closed first and last Mon of each month; entrance fee). The gardens are entered from the courtyard via a flight of steps that leads to a terrace to the rear of the palace, in front of Susini's fountain, constructed in 1641. The fountain sits at the focal point of an amphitheatre of grass, laid out in 1630–35 on the site of the quarry that was the source of the stone used to build the Pitti Palace.

It served as an open-air theatre in 1661

Right: Lorenzi's impressive Neptune Fountain in the Boboli Gardens

for the masques and fireworks in celebration of the marriage of Cosimo III to Margaret Louise of Orleans. The huge granite basin nearby is from the ancient Caracalla baths in Rome. A series of terraces leads up to Stoldo Lorenzi's Neptune Fountain (1565–69) and to the left is the little baroque **Kaffeehaus** (open 10am–5.30pm, closed Dec and Jan), built in 1776. The interior is frescoed with garden scenes, and the intimate terrace alongside, which offers a glorious view over Florence, is a perfect spot to reflect on the history of the gardens over a drink or lunch. Above the Kaffeehaus, you can see the imposing walls of **Forte Belvedere**, which was built by Duke Fernando in 1590.

Heading back to the gardens, a path leads up and round to the statue of *Abundance*, then to the enclosed **Giardino del Cavaliere**, constructed in 1529 and now almost fully restored. With low box hedges, rose bushes and rural views, this is a delightful place for a rest. It is bordered by the **Museo dell Porcellane** (Porcelain Museum, open Tues–Sat 8.30am–1.50pm and alternate Sundays), containing Sèvres, Meissen and Viennese ceramics.

Walk past the gardeners' houses until you reach the top of the Viottolone, a shady, cypress avenue planted in 1637 and lined with lichen-covered antique statues. The Oceanus Fountain by Giambologna on the Isolotto (Little Island) and the crumbling statues encircling the lake, make this a magical spot.

From the top of the Viottolone, a path takes you back to the east wing of the Pitti Palace via the smaller Palazzina della Meridiana and past the **Grotta di Buontalenti**, a fantastical grotto with copies of Michelangelo's *Four Slaves* set in the four corners. Further inside, you will come across Paris seducing *Helen of Troy* in Vincenzo de' Rossi's erotic sculpture, and, almost out of sight at the rear of the cave, is Giambologna's *Venus* emerging from her bath. Don't miss the statue of the pot-bellied Pietro Barbino, Cosimo I's court dwarf, riding on a turtle, which is located just by the east gate.

The Browning Abode

Back in Piazza Pitti, turn left and look out for **Casa Guidi** at Piazza San Felice 8. The poets, Robert and Elizabeth Browning, lived in this house from 1847, shortly after their secret marriage, until Elizabeth's death in 1861 (open Apr–Nov, Mon, Wed and Fri 3–6pm; admission free).

From here, turn into Via Mazzetta, which leads into Piazza Santo Spirito

where there is a small market each morning from Monday to Saturday. There are many good (and expensive) antique shops nearby, especially around Via Maggio. This part of the city is very different from the historic centre north of the river – bustling, lively and authentically Florentine. Walk along the right-hand side of the square, noting **Caffe Ricchi** (No. 9r) with tables under the trees; you may want to return here for a drink and dinner in the **Trattoria Borgo Antico** (6r). Next door you can watch carpenters producing intricate mouldings for reproduction furniture, while the antique shop **Il Tempo** (1r) sells toys and 1950s memorabilia.

At the head of the square is the church of **Santo Spirito** (open daily 8am–noon, 4pm–6pm, except Wed afternoon; admission free). This church, which was begun in 1436, was regarded as Brunelleschi's masterpiece and a superb example of Renaissance classicism. Leaving the church, walk up the right-hand side of the square past Osteria Santo Spirito (16r), another potential spot for dinner, with an imaginative menu and wonderful salads.

Cappella Brancacci

Turn right in Via Sant'Agostino, past tempting food shops, and continue down Via Santa Monica to reach the huge **Piazza del Carmine**. The church of Santa Maria del Carmine was destroyed by fire in 1771 and subsequently rebuilt. However the **Cappella Brancacci**, just to the right, was spared (open Mon, Wed–Sat 10am–5pm, Sun 1–5pm; entrance fee). Once inside this tiny chapel you are brought face to face with the newly restored frescoes on the *Life of St Peter*, which were begun by Masolino, continued by Masaccio from 1425 until his death in 1428 and completed by Filippino Lippi in 1480. Masaccio's contribution has been hailed as a superb example of the emerging Renaissance style, remarkable for the clearly worked-out perspective and the use of *chiaroscuro*, light and shade, to highlight the central figures. St Peter, a serene figure, moves among the poor and crippled, distributing alms and working miracles, against the backdrop of the streets and buildings of 15th-century Florence. Masaccio's work is mainly in the upper tier of the fresco and includes his *Expulsion from Paradise*, in which the figures of Adam and Eve, no longer beautiful as in Masolino's *Temptation* scene opposite, are racked with misery. The scenes in the lower tier, mostly by Filippino Lippi, are equally distinguished.

Left: eating *al fresco*. **Above:** making furniture the traditional way. **Right:** pot-bellied Barbino

4. THE BARGELLO AND SANTA CROCE *(see map, p45)*

This morning's visit is to an outstanding collection of sculpture in the Bargello Museum; you can also sample the world's best ice-cream and visit the tombs of Galileo, Machiavelli and Michelangelo.

Start in the **Piazza di San Firenze** with a coffee in the tiny **Bar Nazionale** (No. 7r); your breakfast companions are likely to be lawyers who work in the law courts of the **Tribunale**, the baroque building on the opposite side of the bustling square. First, make a quick detour to the **Badia Fiorentina**, the church opposite the Bargello on the corner of Via dei Proconsolo and

Via Dante Alighieri (currently under restoration; open Mon 3–6pm; admission free; check with the tourist office if renovation has been completed). The church of a Benedictine abbey, founded in 978, but considerably altered in 1627–31, it merits a visit on account of a delightful painting by Filippino Lippi, the *Apparition of the Virgin to St Bernard* (1485) just inside the door. The church's other attraction lies through a door immediately to the right of the high altar; if it is open, walk up the stairs to the peaceful **Chiostro degli Aranci** (named after the orange trees that once grew here). The lovely cloister, adorned with damaged 15th-century frescoes depicting the miracles of St Bernard by Rossellino, offers fine views of the Badia's six-sided Romanesque campanile.

Above: the formidable bulk of the Bargello
Left: reading up on the museum's exhibits

The Bargello

Leave the Badia and cross to the **Bargello** (open daily 8.15am–1.50pm, closed first, third, fifth Sun, second and fourth Mon each month; entrance fee), begun in 1255 as the city's town hall but later used as a prison, as the names of the surrounding streets remind us. Via dei Malcontenti (Street of the Miserable) was the route taken from the Bargello to the gallows. The inner courtyard, where criminals were once executed, is now a peaceful spot, the walls studded with carved armorial stones. The room on the right contains a rich collection of 16th-century sculpture; Michelangelo's first great work, the *Drunken Bacchus* (1499), seems to stagger off his pedestal.

A stately external staircase leads up to the first floor loggia where there is an amusing display of bronze birds made by Giambologna for the grotto of the Medicis' Villa di Castello *(see page 59)*.

The vast hall on the right contains Donatello's *St George* (1416), which was commissioned by the Guild of Armourers for their niche on the exterior of Orsanmichele. The same sculptor's erotically charged *David* (1440), wearing not much more than an enigmatic smile, is also here. On the right-hand wall are the two trial panels made by Ghiberti and Brunelleschi, the winner and runner-up respectively in the competition of 1401 to find a designer for the Baptistry doors; both show the *Sacrifice of Isaac*.

The rest of this fine museum is a mixed bag covering everything from Islamic ceramics to coins and armour. Exploring at will you are bound to find something of interest; perhaps the 6th-century Lombardic jewellery or the rich Persian carpets displayed on this (first) floor, or the sculptures by Verrocchio on the floor above.

Leaving the Bargello, turn left, then first left down Via della Vigna Vecchia. At the second turning to the right look for the **Bar Vivoli Gelateria** (Via Isola delle Stinche 7r, closed Monday), a tiny ice-cream parlour that attracts huge crowds for its imaginative home-made concoctions.

Santa Croce

From here it is a short walk down Via dei Lavatoi, then right, into the huge square fronting **Santa Croce** (open in summer, Mon–Sat 8am–5.45pm; winter, Mon–Sat 9.50am–5.45pm, Sun 3–5.30pm; admission free), the magnificent Gothic burial place of many famous Florentines. On the right of the entrance door you will find Michelangelo's tomb, carved by Vasari, Dante's empty sarcophagus (he refused to return to the city that sent him into exile and he is buried in Ravenna), and the graves of the statesman Niccolò Machiavelli, the humanist Leonardo Bruni, and the composer Rossini.

The Bardi Chapel (to the right of the high altar) is covered in frescoes depicting the *Life of St Francis*, once thought to be by Giotto and now attributed to his pupil, Taddeo Gaddi. The corridor on the right leads past the sacristy to a chapel holding Galileo's now empty grave. His body was moved to the north aisle of the church in 1737 when his contention that the sun was at the centre of the universe was no longer considered a heresy.

Outside, to the left, is the **Museo dell'Opera di Santa Croce** (open in summer Thur–Tues 10am–7pm; winter 10am–6pm; entrance fee), with two serene cloisters. The cloister walk leads to the **Capella de' Pazzi**, a noble building of white walls and grey *pietra serena* pilasters, designed by Brunelleschi, which is one of the purest works of the Renaissance.

Above: detail from the door of Santa Croce

city itineraries

5. SANTISSIMA ANNUNZIATA
AND SURROUNDINGS *(see map, p45)*

A half-day tour that includes Brunelleschi's Innocenti orphanage, Santissima Annunziata and the Archaeological Museum.

This morning tour takes in a clutch of little-visited museums and monuments in the north of the city. From Piazza del Duomo, head up Via dei Servi. The street is likely to be busy with traffic and the pavements crowded with Florentines heading for work, but try to find a quiet doorway from which to admire some of Via dei Servi's imposing buildings.

At the first junction, note the **Palazzo Pucci** on the left, home of the late Marchese Pucci and headquarters of his fashion empire. Further up on the left, at No 15, the **Palazzo Niccolini** (1550) is an appropriate headquarters for the Ministry of Public Works – note the *sgraffito* decoration (designs scratched in plaster) and huge overhanging roof sheltering an open loggia.

Via dei Servi leads into the pedestrianised **Piazza della Santissima Annunziata**, which is one of the most beautiful squares in Florence. In the centre of the square is an equestrian statue of Duke Ferdinand I, by Giambologna; this is partnered by two bronze fountains (by Tacca, 1608) featuring strange-looking marine monsters.

On the right-hand side of the square is the gracious colonnade of the **Spedale degli Innocenti**, built by Brunelleschi from 1419 and the first classical loggia of its type. Here the columns of grey *pietra serena* alternate with Luca della Robbia's blue-and-white terracotta roundels depicting a baby in swaddling clothes, the symbol of the Innocenti orphanage just behind. The orphanage, the first in the world (opened in 1444), is still used for its original purpose. It has

a **gallery** of pictures that were donated by patrons, including Ghirlandaio's *Adoration* (open Thur–Tues 8.30am– 2pm; entrance fee). Brunelleschi's portico was copied on the opposite side of the square, where it fronts the entrance to one of the best Florentine hotels, the Loggiata dei Serviti.

Frescoes and Bronzes

On the north side of the square, it forms the grand entrance to the church of **Santissima Annunziata** (open daily 7.30am–12.30pm, 4–6.30pm; admission free). This contains some fine frescoes, such as Andrea del Sarto's *Birth of the Virgin* (1514) and, in the adjacent Chiostro dei Morti (Cloister of the Dead), his *Holy Family*.

Turn right down Via della Colonna at the top right of the square and you will come to the **Museo Archeologico**

Right: a chance to cool off outside the Spedale degli Innocenti

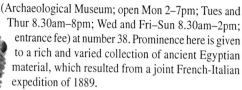

(Archaeological Museum; open Mon 2–7pm; Tues and Thur 8.30am–8pm; Wed and Fri–Sun 8.30am–2pm; entrance fee) at number 38. Prominence here is given to a rich and varied collection of ancient Egyptian material, which resulted from a joint French-Italian expedition of 1889.

The real stars of the museum are the Etruscan bronzes displayed in Room XIV. The 5th-century BC *Chimera (pictured here)*, part-lion, part-goat and part-snake, was discovered in Arezzo in 1554 and was greatly admired by Renaissance bronze-casters, including Benvenuto Cellini, who was entrusted with the restoration of a broken fore-leg. The *Orator* (2nd century BC) was discovered in Trasimeno in 1556. A newly opened wing of the museum is devoted to the Medici collections of fabulous antique, medieval and Renaissance jewellery.

6. THE MUSEO DELL'OPERA DEL DUOMO *(see map, p45)*

In this fine museum, Etruscan and Roman finds join masterpieces of Gothic and Renaissance sculpture in wood, bronze and marble, including Michelangelo's *Pietà*. Allow a whole morning for the visit.

The **Museo dell'Opera del Duomo** (Museum of the Cathedral's Artefacts) (open Mon–Sat 9am–7.30pm, Sun 9am–1.40pm, closed public holidays; entrance fee) is located at the eastern end of the Piazza del Duomo *(see Itinerary 1, page 22)*, in a building set up by Brunelleschi in 1432 as the base from which he supervised the construction of the great cathedral dome. Today, it houses a number of outstanding works of sculpture from the cathedral and the campanile, many of which have been brought indoors to protect them from atmospheric pollution and weathering.

In the first two rooms, you will see Etruscan and Roman funerary urns, finds from the excavation that took place in the area between the cathedral and the Baptistry in 1971–72, and Gothic sculptures that stood above the Baptistry doors, before they were replaced by the present Renaissance sculptures. The next two rooms show sculptures that Arnolfo di Cambio and his assistants carved to adorn the facade and side walls of the Duomo. These statues formed part of the half-completed 13th-century facade that was finally taken down in 1587.

To assemble this collection of weatherworn Gothic saints and Madonnas, the museum curators scoured private collections all over Europe and museums in Berlin and Rome. Some were found in Florentine gardens and others had long been hidden, unrecognised, in the Opera del Duomo store rooms. This room leads to the Lapidarium, an assemblage of all kinds of carved and inlaid stones, some of which are now recognised as having come from the huge Romanesque baptismal font that filled the centre of the Baptistry until it was dismantled in 1577.

Above: the *Chimera* in the Archaeological Museum

Next comes the courtyard – open to the skies until the glass roof was added as part of the recent modernisation of the museum – which originally served as a working mason's yard. It was here that Michelangelo carved his *David* – originally intended for display in front of the cathedral. Now the courtyard is home to five of the original 10 panels from the Baptistery Gates of Paradise (the others are still being restored).

The mezzanine floor is devoted to one single work of art – Michelangelo's *Pietà*, begun *circa* 1550 and originally intended to adorn his own tomb. The tall, hooded figure at the centre of the group is a self-portrait – Michelangelo cast himself as Nicodemus, the rich man who donated his tomb for the burial of Christ. The rather stiff figure of Mary Magdalene, to the left, was carved by one of Michelangelo's pupils. Dissatisfied with his work, the great master broke up the *Pietà*; it survived only because a servant kept the pieces.

On the first floor of the museum there are two fine *cantorie* (choir galleries), carved in marble, which were removed from the cathedral during the 17th century. Both depict young musicians in a frenzy of dancing and musicmaking. They were made by two of the leading artists of the day, Donatello and Luca della Robbia, between 1431 and 1438. Here, too, you will find Donatello's powerful *Mary Magdalene*, a figure of penitence carved in wood.

Beyond, a whole room is devoted to the panels that once adorned the base of Giotto's campanile, some by Giotto, others by Andrea Pisano. In the last room of the museum, Lorenzo Ghiberti's original bronze panels from the Paradise (east) door of the Baptistry are displayed – some are in place, others are being restored. The panels provide an excellent opportunity for visitors to study in close-up the

Above: stone reliefs in the museum
Right: Michelangelo's *Pietà*

work that has come to stand as a symbol of the birth of the Renaissance.

The final section of the museum is concerned with Brunelleschi's achievement in building the dome. Tools, brick moulds, pulleys and scaffolding are used to recreate the appearance of a 15th-century building site. You can also see models and drawings produced over several centuries for the cathedral facade. After years of rivalry and contention, a design was finally chosen – that of Emilio de Fabris. The facade was added in the 1880s, almost 600 years after the building was begun.

7. AROUND THE PALAZZO DAVANZATI *(see map, p45)*

Step inside this beautiful palace for a taste of life in Renaissance Florence before exploring nearby medieval alleys and churches.

The **Palazzo Davanzati**, Via Porta Rossa 13, also known as the **Museo dell'Antica Casa Fiorentina**, is temporarily closed as part of a comprehensive restoration campaign. For the time being, visitors can only see the entrance hall, which has an exhibition on the history of the building and its occupants; check with the tourist office when you visit to find out if more of the building has been re-opened to the public).

Look at the facade first; this dates from the mid-14th century and is a typical example of Tuscan pre-Renaissance architecture. You will see plenty of buildings like this in Siena and other Tuscan cities, but in Florence it is a rarity because of the huge amount of rebuilding that went on from the 15th century. A typical feature is the so-called depressed arch over the doors and windows. The coat of arms is that of the Davanzati family who owned the palace from 1518 until 1538. The open loggia that crowns the palace was added in the 16th century.

Inside is a beautiful courtyard and an elegant stone staircase supported on flying arches. Note, too, the well to the right of the entrance with a pulley system enabling buckets of water to be lifted to each of the five floors – a private water supply was a considerable luxury, since most Florentines were dependent on the water supplied by public fountains, which had to be fetched by bucket. The principal living-rooms lie on the first floor, the *piano nobile*,

where (when the building re-opens) you will find the gorgeously frescoed dining-room, the **Sala dei Papagalli** (Room of the Parrots) after the birds pictured in the borders. The bedchambers on the floors above also have murals, notably the one decorated with scenes from the 13th-century French romance, the *Châtelaine de Vergy*. Although the furnishings in each room – beds, chests and stools – may look sparse, they represent a considerable degree of luxury for the time, as do the private bathrooms

off each room, complete with toilets and terracotta waste pipes. In the kitchen on the top floor you will find a fascinating array of contemporary utensils, including equipment for kneading and shaping pasta.

Exploring the Medieval Alleys

As you leave the palace, look opposite and left to see the remains of a medieval tower-house that is typical of an even earlier style of architecture. Turn right, then right again, in Via Pellicceria, to reach another well-preserved group of medieval structures, the battlemented buildings of the **Palazzo di Parte Guelfa**. This dates from the 13th century and was enhanced by Vasari, who built the external staircase in the 16th century. This palace once served as the headquarters of the Guelph party, one of the political factions whose feuding caused mayhem in the city during the 13th and 14th centuries.

Walk through the covered passage straight ahead and turn right in Via delle Terme (commemorating the former site of the Roman baths), with medieval alleys leading off to the left. Take the second left, Via del Fiordaliso, noting the stone *sporti*, or brackets, of the building to the right, supporting the jettied-out upper storeys. Turn right, then take the first left into **Piazza del Limbo**, so called because the site was once used as a burial ground for unbaptised infants whose souls, according to the prevailing Christian dogma, dwelled in Limbo. The church on the left, **Santi Apostoli** (open for services Sat 6–7pm and Sun 8am–1pm), is one of the oldest in the city, dating from about 1050. It incorporates columns salavaged from the Roman baths.

Turn left in Borgo Sante Apostoli and cross busy **Piazza di Santa Trinità** to the church of the same name (open Mon–Sat 8am–noon, 4–6pm, Sun 4–6pm; admission free). Here the relative austerity of the 13th-century Gothic architecture contrasts with Ghirlandaio's stunningly colourful frescoes and altarpiece of the **Sassetti Chapel**, to the right of the choir. The frescoes (1483) illustrate the *Life of St Francis* and the altarpiece (1485) shows the *Nativity*. Other frescoes depict scenes from classical writing and mythology set against a Florentine backdrop, suggesting that Renaissance Florence was conceived as being the new Rome.

Left: the Room of the Parrots
Above: elegant footwear on display in the Palazzo Davanzatti

8. SAN MINIATO AL MONTE *(see map below)*

This somewhat strenuous walk to the jewel-like church of San Miniato and the Piazzale Michelangelo is rewarded by sweeping views over the rooftops of Florence. Allow a leisurely half a day for the round trip.

The lovely Romanesque church of San Miniato al Monte sits on a hill to the south of the city. From **Piazza della Signoria**, walk south through the courtyard of the Uffizi gallery to the Arno embankment and turn left. As you follow the river, look up to the right, where you will see the green-and-white marble facade of San Miniato. The view across the Arno to this church was celebrated in E.M. Forster's novel *A Room With A View* – the room in question was located in the now-defunct Pensione Quisisana.

You can take a bus from the south side of Ponte alle Grazie. Otherwise, cross the bridge and continue until you can go no further, then turn left down Via San Niccolò. This threads past imposing palaces and the church of San Niccolò, up to Via di San Miniato, where you turn right and pass through one of the few surviving arches from the 14th-century city wall.

On the other side of the arch our route goes left, up Via dei Bastoni, which also follows the walls. A short way up, look for a set of stone steps on the right that leads straight uphill, passing through leafy gardens and inter-

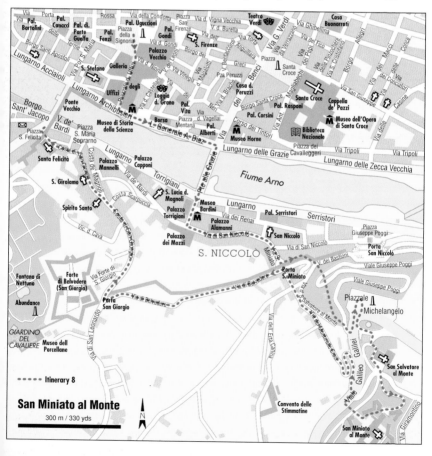

- - - - - Itinerary 8

San Miniato al Monte

300 m / 330 yds

rupted occasionally by the main road. Keep following these steps and paths as they weave uphill; on a clear day, the views are splendid.

When the staircase stops, turn right along the road and look for a gate on the left to the **Giardino delle Rose** (Rose Garden; open daily 8am–8pm; admission free). There is far more here than just roses and plant-lovers will delight in the colourful profusion. Follow the path through the garden and, at the exit, climb the steps to the left to reach the **Piazzale Michelangelo** (if for any reason the garden is closed, continue up the road and look for a path on the right, a short way up). The Piazzale was laid out in the 19th century and the square is dotted with reproductions of Michelangelo's sculptures – not to mention scores of tour buses and souvenir stalls. The views are absolutely marvellous – it is from here that all those classic postcard pictures of the rooftops of Florence are taken.

Turning your back on the Piazzale, head for the **Bar/Ristorante La Loggia**, housed in a 19th-century neoclassical building, where you may want to stop for a lunchtime treat – but be warned, it's fairly expensive.

San Miniato

Keeping to the right of the restaurant, take the flight of steps to the left, which leads to the church of San Salvatore. Follow the path to the right of this church, then take

Above: the delicate facade of San Miniato
Right: the church's rich interior decoration

the left turning towards an arch in the wall surrounding **San Miniato** (open in summer, Mon–Sun 8am–noon, 2–7pm; winter, Mon–Sun 8am–noon, 2.30–6pm; admission free) and its conventual buildings. Catch your breath while admiring the views from the terrace in front of the church and studying its delicate facade, covered in geometric patterns of green-and-white marble.

The church was built on the site of the tomb of the city's first Christian martyr, St Minias. He was executed in AD250 during the anti-Christian purges of the Emperor Diocletian and his shrine was replaced by the present church in 1018. It incorporates Corinthian columns and other Roman materials. Important features inside are the intarsia panels of the floor, now worn, depicting signs of the zodiac; the fragments of 11th- and 12th-century frescoes on the walls; and the raised marble choir and pulpit inset with intarsia panels and depicting mythical beasts. To the left, situated behind an iron grille, is the tomb of the Cardinal of Portugal who died on a visit to Florence in 1439. The mosaic in the apse, of 1297, shows *Christ, the Virgin and St Minias*.

Traditional Wine Bar

With your back to the church facade, descend the stone staircase opposite, passing through the cemetery and noting the fine 19th-century sculptures marking some of the many graves. Cross the road, continue down the next set of steps, cross the road again at the bottom and bear right to find Via del Monte alle Croci on the left. Follow this winding road downhill until you return to the arch in the city wall. On the left is the **Fuori Porta**, one of Florence's best *enoteche* (wine bars). Here, you can choose from an impressive wine list and a menu of excellent savoury snacks.

Once rejuvenated, you can retrace your steps to the city centre, or turn left to follow Via di Belvedere. This involves an uphill climb, following the foot of the city walls, until you reach Porta San Giorgio. Constructed in 1260, this is the city's oldest surviving gate. Alongside the gate is an entrance to the **Forte Belvedere** (currently closed for restoration). Passing beneath the towering fortress walls, go through the Porta San Giorgio and descend the quiet Costa San Giorgio, noting the building at No. 19 which stands on the site of Galileo's home. Where the road forks, take the left-hand route to reach Piazza Santa Felicità, just a few steps from the Ponte Vecchio.

9. FIESOLE *(see map below)*

Escape to the hills for a walk and lunch in the sleepy village that stands less than 6km/4 miles from the centre of Florence. Take bus No. 7 from Santa Maria Novella station or Piazza San Marco, buying your ticket from one of the ticket machines or cafés by the bus stop.

Fiesole is a favourite retreat for Florentines who find the air in this hill-top village fresher and cooler than in the valley bottom where their own city sits. Once, relations between the two towns were not so comfortable. Fiesole predates Florence by some eight centuries; it was an Etruscan city well before the Romans colonised the area and founded the town from which Florence grew. Thereafter, Fiesole declined but remained an important trade competitor until 1125 when Florentine troops stormed it, destroying all the buildings, save for the cathedral.

From the 15th century onwards, numerous fine villas were built on the slopes leading up to Fiesole. Later, they were rented by a growing Anglo-Florentine community which, during the 19th century, included the poets Robert and Elizabeth Barrett Browning. You will see these villas from the bus as you approach Fiesole. The short journey from the city ends at the **Piazza Mino**, Fiesole's broad, main square which occupies the site of the Roman forum.

Left: sculpture in the grounds of Forte Belvedere. **Above:** the Teatro Romano

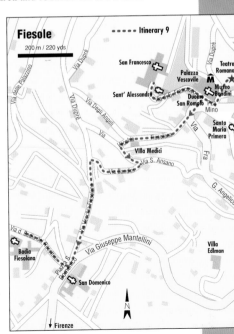

Fiesole
200 m / 220 yds

······· Itinerary 9

Via Dupré
San Francesco
Palazzo Vescovile
Teatro Romano
Museo Bandini
Sant' Alessandro
Duomo San Romolo
Mino
Santa Maria Primera
Via delle Palazzine
Via degli Angeli
Villa Medici
Via S. Ansano
G. Angelico
Fra
Via d.
Badia Fiesolana
Via Giuseppe Mantellini
Villa Edlman
San Domenico

N

↓ Firenze

Cross the square to the entrance to the **Teatro Romano** (open daily in summer, 9.30am–7pm; till 5pm in winter; entrance fee includes admission to the Museo Bandini and Cappella di San Iacopo). This impeccably preserved amphitheatre, with a seating capacity of around 3,000, is the site of a popular arts festival held in July and August *(see Calendar of Events, page 87).*

It enjoys stunning views over the low, cypress-topped hills of the Mugello region to the north. Surrounding the theatre are the jumbled remains of Etruscan and Roman temples and baths. The excellent **Museum Faesulanum**, in the same complex, displays tiny Etruscan figures (dancers, warriors, orators), sensual – but headless – statues of Dionysos and Venus and many other notable sculptures.

Almost directly opposite the entrance to the Teatro Romano, in Via Dupré, the **Museo Bandini** (open in summer, daily 9.30am–7pm; till 5pm in winter; combined entrance fee with the Teatro Romano and Cappella di San Iacopo, as above) has an outstanding collection of paintings by the so-called Italian Primitives – artists who continued to work in the Gothic idiom well into the Renaissance era. Most of the paintings are, by definition, religious, but there is an extremely rare and unusual allegorical work by Jacopo del Sellaio showing the Triumph of Love, Time, Chastity and Piety.

Back on Piazza Mino, turn right to the forbidding **Cattedrale di San Romolo**. This severe, sandstone basilica has 16th-century frescoes in the apse by local artist Nicodemo Ferrucci, on the life of St Romolo, whose sarcophagus is in the crypt below. The jewel of the church is the tomb that Mino da Fiesole designed for the humanistic Bishop Leonardo Salutati.

Look for Via San Francesco, the lane that climbs steeply from the cathedral facade. A short way up is the **Cappella di San Iacopo** (open in summer, daily 9.30am–7pm; till 5pm in winter; combined entrance fee, as above) with a display of ecclesiastical treasures and early crucifixes. Further up, a terrace gives sweeping views over Florence.

At the top of the lane is **Sant'Alessandro**, whose plain, squat facade hides a 6th-century basilica with re-used Roman columns of *cipollino* (onion-ring) marble. Sant'Alessandro is the church of **San Francesco**, constructed on the site of an Etruscan temple. It has been a monastery since the 15th century, and a friendly monk will let you in and allow you to go upstairs and inspect the barren cells in which these holy men spent most of their lives. The church itself is packed with works of art, and there is a curious museum off the cloister, full of dusty relics collected in China and Egypt by Franciscan missionaries.

Why not reward your exertions by having lunch at one of the restaurants in Piazza Mino or, if you prefer, by simply enjoying a relaxing drink and the fine views from the terrace of the lovely Hotel Villa Aurora?

Above: there are fine views of the Florentine countryside
Right: everything in the garden is rosy

Returning to the City

You can now return to Florence by bus or walk part of the way, following the narrow Via Vecchia Fiesolana out of the square. Along the way you will pass the **Villa Medici**, built in 1458, a favourite retreat of Lorenzo de' Medici. You can also enjoy glimpses of other villas behind their high walls and note various examples of stone work, a fountain, lions' heads and the typical Tuscan cypress trees standing sentinel.

The next stop on the route, after 1km (½ mile), is the **Convent of San Domenico**, where you can see Fra Angelico's *Madonna with Angels* (1430) in the church and his *Crucifixion* (1430) in the Chapter House.

From here, you can take the left fork down to the **Badia Fiesolana** – the church that served as Fiesole's cathedral until 1058. The original Romanesque facade, framed by the rough, unfinished stonework of the enlarged 15th-century church, is a delicate work of inlaid marble. There is another magnificent view over Florence from the terrace in front of the church.

Back at the Convent of San Domenico there is a bus stop outside the church where No. 7 bus stops on the way back to Florence.

10. VILLA GARDENS *(see pullout map)*

A visit to two Medici villas with fine gardens in the northern suburbs of the city. Take bus 28A, B or C from the stop to the extreme right of the Santa Maria Novella bus station. Buses leave every 15 minutes or so and tickets can be bought from the machine by the bus-stop.

This tour is a must for garden-lovers – but don't expect colourful herbaceous borders: the two gardens we shall visit today were laid out in the formal Italian style in the 16th century and are of great historical interest. They are open all day, every day except Monday, and can be enjoyed in all seasons. The garden of the Villa della Petraia is backed by extensive woodland which is absolutely perfect for picnicking.

Knowing where to get off the bus is going to be the most difficult part of this tour – befriend someone on the bus, if possible, and ask them to tell you where to get off for the Villa Medicea della Petraia. Alternatively, keep

an eye on the street signs – the bus heads north to the suburb of Rifredi, then follows the railway track along the long Via Reginaldo Giuliani. After about 15 minutes you will pass a power station on the right just before Via Reginaldo Giuliani narrows down to a single lane. Count the house numbers on the right – you want the request stop outside house No. 424.

From there, walk back to house No 292 and turn left up the narrow Via della Petreia. About 500m (⅓ mile) up the lane you will pass the Villa Corsini, with its cream-coloured baroque facade and a plaque recording that Robert Dudley died here on September 6, 1649. Dudley, the illegitimate son of the Earl of Leicester (Queen Elizabeth I's favourite) was the leading marine engineer of his age and was employed by Cosimo I to build the harbour at Livorno, Tuscany's principal port.

The Villa della Petraia

The **Villa della Petraia** is another 1km (⅔ mile) up from here (open Mar–Oct, daily 9am–one hour before dusk, closed second and third Mon of every month; entrance fee includes admission to the Villa di Castello).

Enter the gate and take the first entrance in the wall on the right, passing into the garden that fronts the villa, laid out with low box hedges enclosing flower beds. Take the central path up steps and past a large fish tank to the terrace in front of the villa. From here the scroll work and geometric patterning of the box parterre can best be appreciated. There is a good view from here left to the dome of Florence cathedral, straight ahead to the new industrial suburb of Firenze Nuova and right to the city's Peretola airport.

Individual visitors can wander around the garden at will, but tours of the villa itself are only given to groups of 10, so you may have to wait and team up with other visitors (then press the bell). The main sight inside is the central hallway, covered in frescoes on the history of the Medici. The villa was built in 1575 for Grand Duke Ferdinand I, on the site of an earlier fortress, the tower of which still stands.

During the 19th century, Villa della Petraia was the favourite residence of the King of Italy, Victor Emmanuel II and it was he who had the tree house built in the huge (and now dead) ilex oak to the left of the villa's facade.

To the right of the villa, a gate in the wall leads to a large park full of ilex and cypress trees, dense enough to be cool even in the heat of summer and threaded with little streams. This juxtaposition of the highly formalised garden with wild and mysterious woodland was a favourite, and very effective, device of Italian gardeners.

From the Villa della Petraia, return downhill to the Villa Corsini and turn right, down Via di Castello. Follow this

Left: Villa Petraia, built for Grand Duke Ferdinand I

road, ignoring all side turnings, and you will find the **Villa di Castello** on the right after 500m/⅓ mile (open Mar–Oct, daily 9am– one hour before dusk, closed second and third Mon of every month; combined entrance fee). Turn left at the rear of the villa (not open to the public) to reach the formal garden, laid out for Duke Cosimo I in 1541 and once regarded as the supreme example of Renaissance gardening.

It now lacks some of the features that made it famous – at the back of the garden, the shell-encrusted **Grotta degli Animali** (1579) was once filled with the bronze birds of Giambologna, but these have since been moved to the Bargello Museum *(see page 45)*. Even so, the geometric beds, outlined in box, and the rows of huge terracotta pots containing citrus trees and bougainvillaea are very striking and, viewed from the upper terrace, resemble a vast patterned carpet. Once again, the ordered formality of the parterre contrasts with the wilder woodland above, where the shivering figure of Appennino (by Ammanati) rises from a pool.

To return to Florence, take the villa exit and walk down the avenue opposite. Cross Via Reginaldo Giuliami and walk down Via Fiulio Bechi, then cross the next road, Via Sestesi, and look for the bus stop down on the right

11. The Passeggiata *(see map, p60)*

Flow with the crowds on an early evening stroll around the city, taking in the principal shops, and enjoy just looking at people enjoying themselves.

The *passeggiata*, or evening promenade, is a traditional feature of Italian life. From about 6pm onwards, as most people finish work for the day, everyone pours out onto the central streets of Florence. There they stroll arm-in-arm, stopping to greet old friends and gossip. Some like to window-shop or to buy some last-minute ingredients for supper. Others simply enjoy being out on the street. They stand in groups to discuss – with great animation – appropriate issues in business, politics or even the latest *cause célèbre*.

Watching other people is all part of the fun and in Florence – where locals and foreign visitors intermingle – it is not hard to spot the true Florentines because of the way they dress; looking good *(fare bella figura)* is a matter in which they take great pride. As you join the crowds you will notice some of the main shops of central Florence; their attractive window-displays act as punctuation marks along the way. You may be content to join the window-

Above: sculpture in the undergrowth
Right: creating a *bella figura*

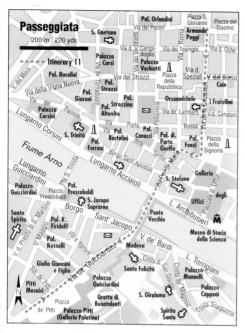

Passeggiata

200 m / 220 yds

- - - - Itinerary 11

shoppers, but you may feel tempted to fit yourself out with a set of new clothes in order to look like an honorary Florentine.

Begin your stroll in **Piazza del Duomo** and head south down Via Calzaiuoli. The first shop on the right, **Armando Poggi** (103r), stocks kitchenware and china, from classic designs to the ultra-modern. This is where many wealthy young Florentines place their wedding lists.

Further down, at **Migone** (85r), you can buy little hand-painted boxes and fill them with a selection of chocolates, bon-bons, marzipan fruits or sweet biscuits. A little way down on the right, **Murano Glass** (41r) is an exotic intruder – the shop sells a huge selection of colourful objects from the famous island of glassmakers in the Venetian lagoon, from jewellery to chandeliers, and from ultra-modern pieces to antique-style wine glasses with gold filigree patterning around the rim.

Opposite, **Coin** (56r) is a fashionable department store, selling chic own-label clothing that does not cost the earth. Ice-creams coming up next: **Pèrche No!** (meaning 'Why Not?') is one of the oldest and best *gelato* makers in the city; the shop is on the left, just after Stefanel, at Via dei Tavolini 19r. Alternatively, you could take the next left (Via dei Cimatori) and join the drinkers on the pavement outside **I Fratellini** (38r) for a glass of Chianti and a couple of crostini at this typical 'hole-in-the-wall' *vinaio*.

Back on the main road, at the entrance to Piazza della Signoria on the right, is **Pineider** (13r); stop to admire (even if you can't afford to buy) the hand-printed stationery, albums, prints and leather briefcases. Wealthy Italians, assorted heads of state and Hollywood stars have their personalised stationery printed here.

At the end of the square, turn right in Via Cacchereccia, past the **Erboristeria** (Herbalist) at No 9r, with its frescoed and beamed interior. Turn left in Via Por Santa Maria and follow the crowds to Ponte Vecchio. Apart from the jewellers' shops and the fast-food restaurants (to be avoided), there will certainly be plenty of street hawkers, mostly sell-

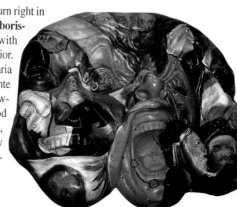

ing imitation Gucci, Prada and Louis Vuitton hand bags. They constantly have one eye out for possible customers and another for the police.

On the way down Por Santa Maria, admire the delicate lace work at **Città di S. Gallo** (60r), the children's party clothes at **Cirri** (40r), or the table linen at **TAF** opposite at 17r – very old-fashioned but also very chic.

Over the Bridge

Once over the Ponte Vecchio, the crowd pushes on south down Via de' Guicciardini. Follow the flow and look out for the **Madova Glove Factory** at No. 1r on the left just over the Ponte Vecchio, which sells exquisite gloves in every shape and colour. **Del Secco** (20r) specialises in lace and hand-embroided linen and **Giulio Giannini e Figlio** (37r) sells marbled papers, notepads, albums and paper sculpture.

A whole arcade at No. 110r is lined with shops selling reproduction Renaissance majolica – everything from tiles to giant vases. If you carry on down to the Pitti Palace, you will find **Pitti Mosaici** at Piazza de' Pitti 37r, occupying the same workshops where the business began in 1858. There is another branch at No. 23r and yet another at No. 16r; all three keep alive the ancient Florentine art of making tables with *trompe-l'oeil* designs out of inlaid marble and semi-precious stones. A little way beyond, **Firenze of Papier-Mâché** (No. 10r) makes everything from carnival masks to painted murals.

At this point it is time to turn back and swim against the flow of human bodies to reach Piazza della Signoria. Here take a seat and a well-earned rest at **Rivoire**, the café offering the best view of the square. You can relax and watch the buskers, the human statues, the crowds, the greedy pigeons and the horse-drawn carriages as you drink a cup of iced chocolate or sip an aperitif. If you have any money left after your shopping trip, you might want to take away a tiny box of Rivoire's delectable hand-made chocolates as a souvenir.

Left: an exotic mask for sale
Above: there are plenty of inexpensive reproductions

Excursions

1. PISA   *(see map, p65)*

Visit the world-famous Leaning Tower, the Cathedral, Baptistry and Camposanto on a day trip from Florence. The trip can be easily made in a day and the main sights do not close at lunchtime.

Many visitors to Florence arrive and depart from Pisa's Galileo Galilei airport, but do not find time to visit Pisa itself. This is a pity, since Pisa is very easy to reach from Florence and its sights are memorable. Trains for Pisa depart from **Santa Maria Novella** station in Florence roughly every hour every day of the week and the fare is very cheap.

The train follows the Arno valley downstream, calling first at the industrial town of Empoli, before arriving at Pisa Centrale station after 53 minutes. Alight here and leave the station, heading straight up Viale Gramsci, crossing the busy Piazza Vittorio Emanuele and continuing up Corso Italia. This brings you to the banks of the Arno River, much wider here than in Florence and bridged by the Ponte di Mezzo. Cross to Piazza Garibaldi and walk up the arcaded Borgo Stretto, Pisa's animated main shopping street. Take the first left, Via Dini, to reach the **Piazza dei Cavalieri** (Square of the Knights).

This square is dominated by the **Palazzo della Carovana**, built by Vasari in 1562 and covered in black and white *sgraffiti* decoration, featuring signs of the Zodiac and mythical figures. The palazzo (now a high school) stands on the site of Pisa's original *municipio* (town hall), which was demolished in 1509 to symbolise the subjugation of Pisa after the city had been defeated by the powerful Florentines.

A large and domineering statue of Duke Cosimo I stands in front of the palace. To the right of the building is the church of Santo Stefano, which contains war trophies captured by the crusading *cavalieri* (knights) of St Stephen in battles against the Turks.

To the left is the **Palazzo dell Orologio** (Palace of the Clock), which incorporates the grim Torre Gualandi, known as the Tower of Hunger. This is where Count Ugolino, along with all his sons and grandsons, was walled up and starved to death in 1288 for allegedly betraying Pisa to the Genoese. The tragic story is told both in Dante's *Inferno* (Canto XXXIII) and in Shelley's poem, *The Tower of Famine*.

Left: the amazing Leaning Tower
Right: Cosimo I stands in front of the palace

Pass under the arch beneath the clock tower and take the right-hand street, Via Martiri. This bends left to join Via San Giuseppe, which leads to the **Campo dei Miracoli** (Field of Miracles) where the bizarre ensemble of Pisa's Leaning Tower, the Cathedral and the Baptistry is revealed. No matter how many photographs you may have seen, nothing prepares you for the impact of these extraordinary buildings when seen at first hand.

Pisa was a thriving port until the mouth of the River Arno silted up, and the city had extensive trade contacts with Spain and North Africa during the 12th and 13th centuries – hence the Moorish influence on the architecture of these buildings, evident in the marble arabesque patterns that cover the walls of the Cathedral and the bristling, minaret-like pinnacles of the Baptistry. All of the buildings tilt, not just the Leaning Tower, so you are likely to experience sensations of vertigo if you look at them for too long.

The ticket office for these buildings is to the right, beside the Leaning Tower. Various combinations are on offer, depending on which monuments you want to visit, and there's a good-value, all-inclusive ticket.

The Tower and the Duomo

The **Leaning Tower**, begun in 1173, started to tilt during the early stages of construction, when it was only 10.5 metres (35ft) high. Some people like to joke that the Pisans deliberately built it this way so as to ensure a healthy income from tourism in years to come. Completed in 1350, the tower has continued to slide, and now, at 54.5 metres (180ft) high, it leans 4.5 metres

(15ft) from the perpendicular. An ambitious 300-billion-lire underpinning programme has recently been completed and has been pronounced a success. It is envisaged that small numbers of visitors will once again be allowed to climb the tower at some stage in the future.

The **Duomo** (Cathedral; open Mon–Sat 10am–7.40pm, Sun 1–7.40pm) alongside the tower is as interesting for its exterior as its interior. It was begun in 1063 and the facade is covered in rising tiers of colonnades, typical of the distinctive Pisan Romanesque style. The bronze doors below these colonnades date from 1602 and illustrate biblical scenes. The Cathedral is entered through the south transept, which also has important Romanesque bronze doors, designed by Bonnano da Pisa in 1180 and illustrating scenes from the *Life of Christ*.

Left: the distinctive colonnaded facade of the Duomo

excursions

Fire devastated the interior in 1595 but spared Cimabue's mosaic of *Christ in Majesty* (1302) in the vault of the apse and Giovanni Pisano's outstanding pulpit, carved with New Testament scenes. The work of the father-and-son team, Nicola and Giovanni Pisano, transcends art-historical categories. Although working in the 13th century, when Gothic was the predominant style, their output anticipates the best Renaissance sculpture of the following century. You will see more of it in the **Baptistry** (open daily 8am–8pm; entrance fee includes access to the dome, from which there are unusual views of the surrounding monuments). The Baptistry was designed and completed by the Pisani in 1284 and contains Nicola Pisano's fine pulpit, his first great work, its panels carved with animated scenes from the *Life of Christ*.

Giorgio Vasari, the great 16th-century art historian, tells us that the Pisani were influenced by the carvings on the Roman sarcophagi that are to be found in the **Camposanto** (Holy Field; open daily 8am–8pm), the cemetery that lies to the north of the Cathedral, enclosed by marble walls. This was begun in 1278, and shiploads of soil were brought back from the Holy Land in Pisan ships, along with the sarcophagi, to add sanctity to the burial ground.

The cloister walls surrounding the cemetery were once gloriously frescoed, but they were seriously damaged when a stray Allied bomb hit the cemetery in 1944. Even so, fragments remain of a lively *Last Judgement* by an unknown 14th-century artist.

Above: an illustrated manuscript in the Museo dell'Opera del Duomo

On the opposite side of the Campo dei Miracoli is the **Museo delle Sinopie** (open daily 8am–8pm), which is where the remaining frescoes from the Camposanto were taken and are now on display. The museum's name is an apt one because many of the frescoes consist of nothing more than the *sinopie*, the preliminary designs sketched into the plaster undercoat to guide the artist during the final stage – painting the finished fresco on to the moist final coat of plaster.

Perhaps more interesting is the **Museo dell'Opera del Duomo** (open daily 8am–8pm) on the corner of the Piazza del Duomo nearest to the Leaning Tower. This museum contains numerous works of art, including Giovanni Pisano's exquisite *Virgin and Child* carved in ivory, and there is also an unusual view of the Leaning Tower to be had from the museum courtyard.

Romanesque and Gothic Churches

You can retrace your steps back to the station from here if you want to go straight back to Florence, or extend your trip by taking a slightly longer route, via two churches with exceptional exterior decoration. From Piazza del Duomo, take Via Roma southwards, passing the Orto Botanico (Botanical Garden), to the Arno embankment. Turn right along Lungarno Simonelli and cross the next bridge, then turn left to reach the church of **San Paolo a Ripa d'Arno**, which has another splendid Pisan Romanesque facade.

Further down the Arno embankment is the church of **Santa Maria della Spina**, covered with prickly pinnacles and niches containing statues of Christ, the Virgin and the Apostles. This 14th-century Gothic church was built to house a single thorn from Christ's Crown of Thorns. This theme is picked up in the bristling exterior and gives the church its unusual name.

A right turn here will take you down Via Sant'Antonio and back to Pisa Centrale station, from where hourly trains will take you back to Florence.

Above: time for a chat in the Piazza dei Cavalieri

2. LUCCA *(see map, p68)*

Visit a walled Tuscan city packed with churches, museums, cafés and shops on an easy day trip by train from Florence – the journey time is around 90 minutes.

Lucca is a perfect example of the Italian concept of *vivabilitá* – liveability – a characteristic that many would argue Florence has lost. The city and its squares are an extension of the home. The people of Lucca go out into the streets to meet friends, and enjoy the city's charms, to eat at pavement cafés in traffic-free streets, and to hear baroque chamber concerts, opera or rock music performed throughout the summer in squares and churches all over the city. To share in this city's delightful atmosphere, take one of the several trains that depart each day from Santa Maria Novella station in Florence, which take around 90 minutes to get to Lucca. Exit Lucca station, and walk in as

straight a line as possible across the station piazza, across a main road and along a path that heads for the city's towering and formidable bank of red-brick walls.

A small underpass takes you through, then up onto the walls, which were built from 1500 and proved very effective in keeping Lucca's enemies at bay. Unlike Siena and Pisa, Lucca did not succumb to the military might of Duke Cosimo I, and the city remained independent until 1847, when it voluntarily became part of the newly created Kingdom of Italy.

In 1817, the massive ramparts were planted with a double row of plane trees, which now shade the broad avenue that follows the line of the walls. This is used by Lucca's citizens as a playground, a jogging and cycle track and a promenade, specially for the evening *passeggiata*.

We descend from the walls to walk around to the front of the **Duomo di San Martino** (open daily 7am–6.30pm, till 5.45pm on public holidays; admission free). The Cathedral's striking facade is decorated with a sculpture of St Martin dividing his cloak (the original sculpture is now just inside the church, on the west wall). The whole surface is decorated with the inlaid marble designs that typify the Tuscan Romanesque style: hunting scenes figure large, with dogs, boars, and huntsmen on horseback, some carrying hawks, some with spears. Flanking the central portal are scenes of the Labours of the Months, and the Miracles of St Martin.

Above: the Romanesque arches of San Martino
Right: beasts adorn the facade of the church

This vivid picture of medieval life and preoccupations is complemented inside by the domed *tempietto* in the nave that contains a magnificent, larger-than-life Crucifixion in carved and painted wood. The face of Christ – with high cheekbones, big eyes and divided beard – is also typically Romanesque and far from realistic, but medieval kings and pilgrims sincerely believed that this was a true and accurate portrait of Christ, carved by Nicodemus, who witnessed the Crucifixion. The Volto Santo (Holy Face) arrived miraculously in an unmanned ship, and landed on the coast near Lucca.

The fame of Lucca's Holy Image spread far and wide and spawned some fascinating linguistic corruptions. St Vaudeluc, worshipped in parts of Central France, is derived from a misinterpretation of the words, *Saint Vault de Lucques*. The bearded, crucified Virgin, Santa Kummernis, worshipped in parts of Germany, may have resulted from crude copies of the Volto Santo, made by village carpenters. When taking solemn vows, the English king, William II, could think of no more holy an object to swear by than the '*sanctum Vultum de Lucca*'.

The **Sacristy** is situated off the south aisle (open Mon–Fri 9.30am–5.45pm, Sat till 6.45pm, Sun 9–9.50am, 11.20–11.50am and 1–6.15pm; entrance fee: combined ticket also allows admission to the Museo della Cattedrale and the church of Santi Giovanni e Reparata). It contains another celebrated image: the tomb of Ilaria del Carretto (died 1405), a masterpiece of realistic carving by Jacopo della Quercia. Ilaria was the wife of the then ruler of Lucca, Paolo Guinigi; she died two years after their marriage, at the age of 24, after the birth of their second child. The tender portrait in marble shows her in a wide-brimmed headdress that frames her beautiful head, with a dog at her feet, symbolising fidelity.

Immediately north of the cathedral is the **Museo della Cattedrale** (open daily 10am–6pm; combined entrance fee – see Sacristy, above), where you will get a free audio guide that provides background information on exhibits that range from rare 6th-century ivory and wax writing tablets, to the festive costumes and jewellery that are used to dress up the Volto Santo when it is carried in procession around Lucca on 13 September every year.

Coming out of the museum, turn right and walk across the Cathedral square, past the 16th-century Palazzo Michaletti, into the next square and the church of **Santi Giovanni e Reparata** (open daily 10am–6pm; combined entrance fee – see Sacristy, above). The now-redundant church has been comprehensively excavated; beneath the modern floor is a

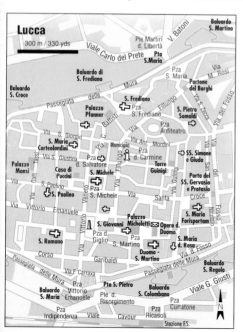

wealth of Roman and medieval structures. The earliest is a 1st-century BC mosaic floor, part of a house that was superseded by a 2nd-century AD Roman bath house, which gave way to a 5th-century baptistry, later joined by a series of churches, culminating in the present 12th-century building.

One of the most intriguing exhibits in the church is a plaster wall scratched with 12th-century graffiti referring to the legend of St Reparata. These show angels carrying the head of the martyred girl, who was beheaded in Palestine in the 3rd century AD, and placing it in a boat. The knight on horseback is the Prince of Benevento, in Campania, who found the martyr's remains when the boat washed up on his shores, and built a shrine to contain them.

Restaurants and Museums

With lunch in mind, leave the church and take the left-hand exit on the opposite side of the square (Via del Duomo), which brings you to the Piazza del Giglio, home to the city's theatre and opera house, the **Teatro Comunale del Giglio**. Adjoining the square to the right is the much larger Piazza Napoleone, with its central statue of Maria Luisa Bobbonai, the 19th-century ruler of Lucca, looking across to the 16th-century Palazzo Ducale. The eastern side of the square, shaded by tall plane trees, has a choice of outdoor restaurants. The **Ristorante del Teatro** (Piazza Napoleone 25, tel: 0583 493 740, closed Tues) is a great place for a long and leisurely seafood lunch (seafood salad, grilled seafood or seafood risotto), or you can have simple pasta in Lucchese pesto sauce (Lucca is rightly proud of the quality of its local-grown basil, from which pesto is made). If you don't want a full meal, try **Bar Pacini** next door for salads or sandwiches; or its neighbour, the **Pizzeria Fuori la Piazza**, for delicious thin-crust pizzas.

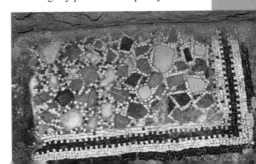

Above and Right: excavations beneath Santi Giovanni e Reparata

Heading north out of the square takes you past stalls selling old engravings and second-hand books, into Piazza San Michele, ringed by Renaissance arcades. At the centre of the square, **San Michele** church (closed) has a facade to rival that of the Cathedral, featuring hunting scenes in green-and-white marble, with animals both exotic (bears, dragons and elephants) and domestic (a rabbit, a duck and a crow eating grapes). Turning your back on the facade, take an alley called Via di Poggio past the **Casa Museo Puccini** (Corte San Lorenzo 9; open daily 10am–6pm; entrance fee), the birthplace of Lucca's celebrated operatic composer, Giacomo Puccini (1858–1924).

Palazzo Mansi

Continue down Via di Poggio, then right into Piazza del Palazzo Dipinto and left down Via del Toro. If you have navigated successfully through Lucca's maze of medieval alleys you will now be at the Palazzo Mansi, in Via Galli Tassi, which houses the **Museo e Pinacoteca Nazionale** (open Tues–Sat 8.30am–7.30pm, Sun and holidays 8.30am–1.30pm; entrance fee). Deities and allegorical figures romp across the ceilings of this splendidly furnished 17th-century home of Cardinal Spada (1659–1724), which features the paintings of Pietro Paolini (1603–81), a local artist specialising in the use of vivid lighting effects to heighten the drama of his works.

Upstairs, at the end of a sequence of rooms decorated round the theme of the Four Elements, is a sumptuous bedchamber dedicated to Fire. This fire is not a destructive flame but the fire that is ignited when Eros strikes with

Above: filling up at a fountain, Lucca

excursions

his arrow, and the room features a gorgeous double bed, with lovely bed and hangings decorated with birds and flowers.

Turn left out of the museum, in Via Galli Tassi, first right in Via San Giustina, and all the way down past fine palaces to Piazza del Salvatore, with its graceful fountain and 12th-century church. Continue for two more blocks and you will reach Via Fillungo, the city's main shopping street. You join the street at Piazza dei Mercanti, where the old, covered market is now a stylish café, the **Loggia dei Mercanti** (No. 42). The street has many fine shop fronts dating from the turn of the 19th and 20th centuries. One of them – the **Perfumeria Venus** – is opposite the café (at No. 65), its art nouveau facade decorated with an ecstatic dancing Venus carved in marble.

With your back to this shop, go straight down Via Sant'Andrea, heading for the red-brick tower that you can see at the end of the lane, distinctive because of the trees growing out of the top (open daily 9am–7.30pm; entrance fee). Dating from the 14th-century, this is a rare survival of a defensive tower, built as a status symbol and as a place of retreat in times of trouble; the tower is of a kind that was once commonplace in medieval Tuscany. If you climb it, as well as views of the nearby countryside you will also see the outline of Lucca's Roman amphitheatre, perfectly preserved in the buildings that were constructed up against it in the Middle Ages.

For a closer look at this remarkable egg-shaped piazza, turn right out of the tower, then first right in Via delle Chiavi d'Oro. Passing the art-deco public baths (now a cultural centre), keep going until you reach the curving wall of the **Anfiteatro**. Ringed by cafés and souvenir shops, the amphitheatre is an atmospheric place to enjoy a bowl of fresh fruit or ice-cream, or linger on for dinner if you are getting a late train back to Florence.

If you exit through the archway opposite the one you entered, and follow the curve of the amphitheatre to the left, you will return to Via Fillungo, close to the church of **San Frediano**, with its huge gold and blue facade mosaic of Christ in Majesty. The treasure of this church is its Romanesque font, as big as a fountain and carved with scenes showing Moses and his entourage of camels, leading his people (dressed in armour) through the divided Red Sea.

To the rear and left of the church is the **Palazzo Pfanner** (Via degli Asili 33; open daily 10am–6pm; entrance fee), a delightful 17th-century resi-

dence used as a location for the filming of Jane Campion's (1996) version of Henry James's novel *A Portrait of a Lady*. You can get a free, sneak view of the wonderful garden and exterior staircase at the rear of the palace by climbing onto the city walls at the rear of San Frediano church and walking left for a short distance.

Back at San Frediano, turn right down Via Fillungo and keep straight on all the way back to the city walls and the railway station.

Right: the amphitheatre is an attractive place to stop for a drink

Leisure Activities

SHOPPING

Some visitors come to Florence simply to shop and even for those of lesser means, window-shopping can be fun. There are some genuine bargains to be found if you search diligently, especially in the big street markets around San Lorenzo and the Mercato Nuovo.

High fashion in Via de' Tornabuoni

Although Milan claims to be the world capital of *haute couture*, Florence has its fair share of home-grown designers of international repute. Nearly all have their outlets at the southern end of Via de' Tornabuoni, the upmarket shopping area. The exception is **Emilio Pucci**, famous for his sexy underwear and for inventing the trouser suit (known as palazzo pyjamas when trouser suits were all the rage as evening wear in the 1960s). Marchese Pucci lived in an ancestral palace, designed by Ammanati, at Via de' Pucci 6. The Pucci boutique is around the corner at Via Ricasoli 36r.

A tour of Via Tornabuoni should start at the southern end, walking up the right-hand side of the street. The huge 13th-century building on the right is Palazzo Spini Ferroni, home to the **Ferragamo** boutique. Neapolitan Salvatore Ferragamo was born into poverty but became known as the 'shoemaker to the stars' while working in Hollywood. Still a family-run business, the shop sells clothes, accessories and soft furnishings, as well as the world-famous footwear. There is a museum in the palazzo (open Mon–Fri 9am–1pm, 2–6pm by appointment only; tel: 055 3360456), which is a testament to Ferragamo's work.

Continuing up the street, you will find **Trussardi** at No. 36r, followed by **Cartier** at No. 40r, beyond the Palazzo Strozzi. Pop into the old-fashioned bar and grocers' shop, **Procacci** (No. 64r) for a *panino tartufato* (a truffle-filled sandwich) and a glass of

prosecco (a dry, sparkling wine, drunk as an aperitif) before reaching the excellent **Seeber** bookshop (No. 68r). Have a look at the contemporary paintings for sale at the **Galleria Tornabuoni** (No. 74r) and at the leather-bound diaries and smart stationery at **Pneider** (76r).

Next comes the baroque bulk of San Gaetano church; cross here to have a look at the Palazzo Antinori, with its celebrated wine bar. Heading back towards the river, pass **Hermès** and take a look at the finely embroidered nightwear and linens at **Loretta Caponi**. Next comes the delightful **Erboristeria Inglese**, a perfumery and homeopathic pharmacy housed in the 16th-century Palazzo Lardarel. Classic footwear and bags are to be found in Tod's (103r), then on to **MaxMara**, where chic *alta moda* designs are more affordable than in most of the other shops in this street.

After **Giocosa**, the snack bar and confectioners', turn right down Via della Vigna Nuova for some more fashion heavyweights. Keeping to the right-hand side of the road, **Massimo Rebecchi's** shops (men's fashions at No. 18r and ladies' at 26r) are good for younger, trendy styles. **Furla** (No. 28r) has contemporary bags and **Emilio Cavallini** (No. 24r) can supply tops, tights and stockings in all sorts of bizzare colours and styles. At the far end of the street, by the Loggia dei Rucellai, **Ermenegildo Zegna** is the place to find smart menswear before drool-

Left: Salvatore Ferragamo's elegant boutique
Above: Florence is a good place to buy shoes

ing at the understated elegance in **Giorgio Armani's** store (Nos 49–53r). **Valentino** is virtually next door. **Dolce & Gabbana** is at Nos 23–25r, followed by **La Perla** (No. 17r). The first of several **Gucci** shops (now less 'scarves and stirrups' than cool black) is at Nos 7–13r. By contrast, you could have a look at some of the many rare antique books and prints for sale at **Ippogrifo** (No. 5r). Terminating this street of chic is **Enrico Coveri**, a designer who specialises in the use of blindingly vibrant colours.

Back on Via Tornabuoni, Gucci's flagship store is at No. 79r, closely followed by **Prada**, one of the extraordinary fashion successes of the late 1990s. **Bulgari's** elegant designs are to be found at Nos 61–63r, while **YSL** is at No. 31r.

If you have bought more than you had planned, you might want to splash out on a suitcase by **Louis Vuitton** (Nos 26–28r) to help you carry it all home. Whatever you do, don't miss **Versace's** glamorous creations at No. 15r.

Food, fashion and fabrics in the city centre

Two blocks west of Piazza del Duomo, at Via dei' Vecchietti 28r, is the **Old England Stores**, a long, narrow shop lined with glass-fronted cabinets selling everything British from breakfast cereals and Fortnum & Mason marmalade to cashmeres and tweed. Its existence bears witness to the fact that some Florentines hold certain British products in high regard.

Heading east towards Piazza del Duomo, do not miss **Casa dei Tessuti** at Via de' Pecori 20–24r; this textile shop is piled up to the ceiling with gorgeous (and costly) antique-style fabrics, rich enough to grace a Renaissance palace.

By contrast, **Max Mara** opposite (No. 23r) is full of bold but stylish clothes. Turn right down Via Roma for **Luisa** (No. 21r), a boutique that stocks clothes designed by the likes of Issey Miyake, Comme des Garçons and Jean-Paul Gaultier. **Eredi Chianini** opposite (No. 16r) is a very masculine shop, selling everything from jeans and aftershave to silk underwear. Further down, **Gilli** (No. 3r) is renowned for its hand-made chocolates and perfect pastries.

Heading down Via Calimala, you will soon come to the crowded **Mercato Nuovo**, built in 1547 and packed with stalls selling leather goods, lace, costume jewellery and T-shirts. Look out for inexpensive soaps, perfumes and

Above: luxurious handwoven textiles

fragrances at the **Erboristeria della Antica Farmacia del Cinghiale** (Via Calimala 4r) alongside the market.

Going for Gold

Jewellers have been operating from the Ponte Vecchio since the 16th century. Sadly, much of what is sold on the bridge today is mass-produced in factories elsewhere and geared to the tourist's desire to find an appropriate souvenir to take home.

Before you get to the bridge, you will find some of the more creative jewellers. At Via Por Santa Maria 1r, is **Bijoux Cascio**, selling good chunky (gold-plated) jewellery at affordable prices. On the left-hand side at the start of the bridge is **Ristori** – look for the fabulous display in the window (but if you need to ask the price, this shop is probably not for you).

Also worth a look are **U. Gherardi** (next door), which is cheaper and specialises in coral and cultured pearls; and the particularly creative **Piccini** (just before the gap in the middle of the bridge).

On the opposite side of the bridge, you may see crowds outside **Cassetti's**, a shop whose contemporary designs attract admiring Florentines. **S.A.D.A.** (opposite) sells only antique pieces, ranging from cameo brooches to Garrard, Tiffany and Cartier products of a century ago.

Food and drink

The following shops, somewhat off the beaten track, are the best in their class and well worth seeking out. **Alessi**, Via dell' Oche 29r, sells the widest selection of chocolates, biscuits, Tuscan honey and jams, wines and spirits that you will find in Florence. The drinks section alone is a delightful showcase for local wines, spirits and liqueurs; here you can still buy the traditional straw-wrapped flasks of Chianti, and the *grappa vecchia*, produced by Jacopo Poli, is worth buying just for the elegance of the bottle designs.

If you have time, turn right out of Alessi, down to the end of Via dell' Oche, to find more gastronomic treats at **Pegna** (Via dello Studio 28r) – the best place to buy olive oil, balsamic vinegar, sun-dried tomatoes, dried mushrooms and bottled *antipasti*.

Fonte dei Dolci (Via Nazionale 120r) is a fairyland for those with a sweeth tooth: slabs of chocolate in pink, orange, white or green; piles and bundles of brightly coloured packets of candies; nougat, marzipan and chocolate liqueurs – and everything beautifully packaged enough to be a special gift.

Marbled paper

If you want to buy marbled and patterned papers, which are a Florentine speciality, the best selection and keenest prices are to be found at the shops opposite the Pitti Palace, and at **Bottega Artigiana del Libro**, on Lungarno Corsini 40r. Here you can buy sheets of paper, albums, notebooks, carnival masks and paper formed into delicate origami peacocks and flowers. While you are here, don't miss **P. Bazzanti**, further along the embankment, beyond the Palazzo Corsini, at No. 46r. This art gallery stocks bronze and marble reproductions of many Florentine statues – just the place to buy a nymph or deity for the garden.

Markets

Apart from the Mercato Nuovo *(see page 74)*, the big open-air market in the streets around San Lorenzo and around the Mercato Centrale has some splendid bargains in leather goods, woollen jumpers, gloves, shoes and boots. It's not easy to bargain with a Florentine, but try it. A flea market operates every day except Sunday at Piazza dei Ciompi, near Santa Croce. Great bargains can be had here and it's fun for browsing even if you don't buy.

Right: bright bags for summer

Art for sale

Grand Tourists of the 19th century came to Florence to buy Renaissance paintings from dealers and impoverished aristocrats. Renaissance art was deeply unfashionable in the late 18th and early 19th century (until rediscovered by Ruskin and the pre-Raphaelites) and many an English aristocrat was able to buy pictures to furnish a stately home at knockdown prices. Most of the major picture galleries of Europe acquired their artistic treasures in this way.

Where would you go today to buy a picture? You can buy quality engravings, and good modern art, not far from the Piazza della Signoria. From the equestrian statue of Duke Cosimo I, turn your back on the Loggia dei Lanzi, and walk north up Via delle Farine, then right along Via della Condotta.

On the left, you will pass the shop of **V. Nencioni** (No. 36r), selling both antique and modern prints – everything from depictions of Florentine monuments to botanical prints. The shop also has some hand-coloured engravings of Giusto Utens' famous 1599 paintings of Medici villas.

Next door, the shop called **Bizzarri** (No. 32r) looks rather like an old-fashioned chemists: in fact it sells the raw minerals and mineral pigments – as well as ready-made paints – that are used by Florentine art restorers and artists.

Several *cartoleria* follow: these are shops selling handmade paper and fine stationery. **Festina Lente** (No. 14) specialises in reproductions of classical bronzes, as well as modern art; and **Bartolucci** (No. 12) is devoted to toys made of wood by the four members of the Bartolucci family. This is a wonderful place for parents tired of buying their children mass-produced plastic toys.

Coming into Piazza di San Firenze, turn left past the Bargello, and right into Via Ghibellina, traditionally another artisans' quarter. Low rents in this long street leading to Santa Croce mean that it has been colonised by young artists and small galleries in recent years. Walk a short way down here and you will find the **Cornici** poster shop (No. 141r) which stocks a huge range of contemporary posters and views of Florence. Next comes the **Galleria Ficari** (No. 168r) set in a graceful glassed-in loggia, next door to the 15th-century Palazzo Borghese, which exhibits sculpture and paintings by leading contemporary artists.

Several more galleries and picture framers lie further down the street, including the **Galleria d'Arte Spagna** at No. 97r. You are now only a short distance away from one of the best ice-cream parlours in Florence: take the next right, Via dell'Isola delle Stinche, and treat yourself to a delicious ice cream at the famous **Vivoli Gelateria**. This is an extremely popular establishment so be prepared for long queues in summer

EATING OUT

You can eat well and cheaply in Florence on pizza and pasta, or on a simple diet put together from the offerings of street markets or an *alimentari* (grocer). On some occasions nothing can beat a picnic of bread *(pane)*, plump black olives *(olive)*, tomatoes *(pomodori)*, sheep's cheese *(pecorino)*, Tuscan ham *(prosciutto)* and fruits such as figs, apricots or peaches *(fichi, albicocche and pesche)*.

Other occasions and other moods demand a full-blown meal in the Italian style, preferably *al fresco*, in a restaurant with a garden, since eating out in Italy is as much a social event as a gourmet experience. Regulations concerning the spread of BSE ('mad cow disease') have meant that restaurateurs are no longer allowed to sell local beef on the bone, which temporarily dented sales of the Florentine speciality, *bistecca alla fiorentina*. This is a tender, juicy, rib steak, traditionally from cattle raised in the Val di Chiana, grilled over charcoal, fragrant with herbs and served with lemon. Today, the meat is more likely to come from certified BSE-free herds in South America. The menu price is per 100 grams (3½ ounces) of uncooked meat. Some restaurants will only serve the meat rare *(al sangue)*; try asking for *ben cotta* (well done) if that is what you prefer, but be prepared for a polite refusal.

Many restaurants in the more tourist-oriented parts of the city offer 'fixed-price' menus *(prezzo fisso)*; although these may represent good value for money, they are not always the best option, as the result can be quite mediocre. Italian-style fast-food places usually offer pasta, pizza and salads, a pleasant change from hamburgers and hot dogs but hardly the 'real thing'. An alternative for a light and inexpensive lunch is one of the many wine bars (usually called *enoteca* or *vinaio*) in the city, where you can have a satisfying snack (or even a full meal) accompanied by a glass of good wine. As a rule, try to find somewhere to eat that is slightly away from the beaten tourist track.

Basic rules

If you decide to eat in a *ristorante* or a *trattoria* you will be expected to order either a

starter *(antipasto)* or a first course *(primo)* of pasta, rice *(risotto)* or soup *(minestra or zuppa)*, followed by a main course *(secondo)* of meat or fish. This is served without accompaniment; if you want salad *(insalata)* or vegetables, you will have to order additional side dishes *(contorni)*. The meal finishes with either fruit *(frutta)*, cheese *(formaggio)*, dessert *(dolci)* or ice-cream *(gelato)*, followed by a coffee *(caffè* – invariably an *espresso*, unless you request otherwise). No meal would be complete without the red wines of Chianti (if you prefer white, try Vernaccia di San Gimignano), while for a *digestivo*, try Vinsanto, a sweet but complex dessert wine, served with sweet almond-flavoured biscuits *(cantucci)* intended to be dipped into the wine.

Prices

The price categories quoted below are based on the average cost of a three-course meal for two, including cover and service charges, but excluding the cost of drink: $ = up to €40, $$ = €40–70, $$$ = €70.

Accademia

Piazza di San Marco 7r
Tel: 055-217343
The cool and calm Accademia serves a choice of eight delicious salads, using various combinations of leaves, olives, ham, cheese, tomatoes and mushrooms, and offers

Left: art while you wait in the Piazzale Michelangelo
Above: local dishes served with a smile

a special lunch menu featuring seasonal produce. $

All' Antico Ristoro di Cambi
Via S. Onofrio 1r
Tel: 055-217134
This busy, rustic *trattoria* is nearly always full and the clients are mostly Florentines. It serves genuine Florentine food including excellent *bistecca*. You can dine out on the terrace in summer. Closed Sunday and for a week in mid-August. $

Alle Murate
Via Ghibellina 52r
Tel: 055-240618
One of the new generation of Florentine restaurants, Alle Murate serves Tuscan food with a creative twist in a sophisticated, calm atmosphere. There is plenty of choice and an excellent wine list. $$$

Angiolino
Via Santo Spirito 36r
Tel: 055-2398976
A recent facelift has sacrificed some of the old-fashioned appeal of this popular Oltrarno *trattoria*, but the food is good, it is still relatively cheap and it's authentic. Closed Monday. $

Antico Fattore
Via Lambertesca 1r
Tel: 055-288975
Despite the damage it sustained when the Uffizi bomb went off in 1993, the Antico Fattore looks as venerable and as timeless as ever, with caricatures and old engravings on the walls and a menu of Tuscan specialities, including wild boar, pigeon, and spicy sausages with beans *(salsicce e fagioli)*. At the foot of the Torre de' Pucci opposite the restaurant there is a memorial to those who died in the bomb blast. $$

Aurora
Piazza Mino 39, Fiesole
Tel: 055-59100
Take the No. 7 bus to Fiesole, and 20 minutes after setting out, you could be sitting on the bougainvillaea-shaded terrace of the Aurora restaurant, enjoying glorious sunset views of the city. The menu features such tasty rustic dishes as *tagliata con la rucola*– finely sliced beef, grilled and dressed with juniper oil on a bed of rocket – and *coniglio farcito* – wild rabbit stuffed with artichokes. $$$

Baldovino
Via San Giuseppe 22r
Tel: 055-241773
The modern decor makes a refreshing change from that in the majority of Tuscan *trattorias*. Located just off Piazza Santa Croce, it serves anything from a pizza or salad to a full meal. Closed Monday. $–$$

Beccofino
Piazza degli Scarlatti 1r
Tel: 055-290076
One of Florence's newest restaurants and one of its most trendy – the smart set come to enjoy the clean, designer interior and the creative Tuscan food. You can either eat a full meal at the restaurant or choose a lighter snack from the wine bar menu where prices are lower. Good wine list. $–$$$

Bibe
Via delle Bagnese 1r
Tel: 055-2049085
You need transport for the short journey to this above-average rustic *trattoria*, which has a delightful garden for al fresco meals. The choice includes warming, earthy, chick pea and *porcini* mushroom soup and magnificent puddings. Closed all day Wednesday, and Thursday lunchtime. $$

Above: food that looks as good as it tastes
Right: eating out in Lucca's Piazza Napoleone

Boboli
Via Romana 45r
Tel: 055-2336401
A short walk south of the Pitti Palace, this is a good place to sample such traditional Florentine fare as spaghetti with nuts and salami *(con nocci e salsicce)*, with peas and ham *(alla medici)* or with garlic, capers, tomatoes and olives *(alla buttera)*. $

Le Botteghe di Donatello
Piazza del Duomo 28r
Tel: 055-216678
Located next to the Museo dell'Opera del Duomo, the restaurant stands on the site of Donatello's workshop, where he created many of his celebrated sculptures. Now it is one of the best of the pavement restaurants north of the Duomo, all competing to satisfy Cathedral visitors' lunchtime hunger pangs. The eclectic menu covers everything from pizza to squid in garlic sauce or *involtini di manzo* (rolls of stuffed beef). $$

Il Brindellone
Piazza Piatellina 10r
Tel: 055-217879
Just west of the church of Santa Maria del Carmine is this inexpensive *cantinetta*, one of the city's few vegetarian cafés, serving big salads and lots of meat-free pasta sauces. It also serves generous platefuls of *carpaccio*, *prosciutto*, smoked swordfish and *crostini con fegatini* (chicken livers) for carnivores. $

Buca Lapi
Via del Trebbio 1r
Tel: 055-213768
A characteristic Florentine restaurant in the cellars of Palazzo Antinori. The *bistecca alla Fiorentina* here is possibly the best in town, and there is a good range of local wines. Closed Sunday. $$

Buca San Giovanni
Piazza San Giovanni 8
Tel: 055-287612
This typical, hole-in-the-wall, Florentine restaurant, to the west of the Baptistry, has a menu of earthy basics, such as *ribollita* soup or salt cod and chick peas, as well as more refined truffle, asparagus and fish dishes. $$

Caffè Concerto
Lungarno Cristoforo Colombo 7
Tel: 055-677377
The riverside setting and the wood-filled interior makes this restaurant a fine choice for romantics. The food is excellent, too; Tuscan classics are served with a creative flair and the wine list is extensive. Closed Sunday. $$$

Cantinetta Antinori
Piazza Antinori 3
Tel: 055-292234
A showcase for the wines and other products of the Antinori family, one of Tuscany's oldest and most respected wine-makers. A choice of snacks or full meals in the ambience of a 15th-century palazzo. Reservations are advised. Closed Saturday, Sunday, all August and public holidays. $$$

Capocaccia
Lungarno Corsini 12r
Tel: 055-210751
Almost opposite the graceful Ponte Santa Trinità, with the statues of the Four Seasons,

this sandwich bar with a difference is noted for its great range of *panini* – meat, fish and vegetarian – and its generous salads. It is also a favourite haunt of young romantics who come here in the evening to sit on the embankment wall opposite and drink a glass of wine while watching the sun setting over the Arno. On the water below, hundreds of bats skim the surface in search of insects, while swifts wheel and scream overhead. $

La Casalinga
Via de' Michelozzo 9r
Tel: 055-218624
A family-run eatery and still one of the best-value meals in Florence. It is popular with both locals and visitors, who come for the plentiful helpings of good home cooking and for the local colour. $

Cibreo
Via dei Macci 118r
Tel: 055-2341100
A justly famed, elegant yet relaxed restaurant serving the best of Tuscan cuisine. Leave room for the chocolate cake at the end. You pay half as much for much the same menu if you go round the corner and eat in the *trattoria* at the back, entered from Piazza Ghiberti 35r. Closed Sunday, Monday and all August. $$$

Città di Firenze
Lungarno Corsini 4
Tel: 055-217706
Here you can lunch on light salads or sandwiches, take cocktails outside on the embankment, listen to live music in the piano bar, or dress up for a special evening out in the elegant restaurant. Choose carefully from the short but tempting menu and you can eat relatively cheaply: perhaps jumbo shrimps in clam sauce (*gamberone giganti*) or a *lasagnetta ripiena di pesce del mediterraneo* (lasagne made with Mediterranean fish), or octopus on a bed of fried leeks in vinaigrette (*insalata di polpo*). $$–$$$

Coco Lezzone
Via del Parioncino 26r
Tel: 055-287178
A Florentine institution, 'Il Coco' serves up traditional food of the highest quality using fresh, seasonal ingredients in a classic setting. Peasant dishes such as *pappa al pomodoro*, ribollita and *pasta e fagioli* are wonderfully authentic. These can be followed by a fabulous *bistecca*, roast pork with garlic and rosemary or, on Fridays, *baccalà alla Livornese* (salt cod cooked in a rich tomato sauce). The menu warns that the trilling of mobile phones disturbs the cooking of the *ribollita*, and that their Florentine steak is only served rare. $$

Coquinarius
Via delle Oche 15r
Tel: 055-2302153
If you have never sampled an *enoteca* (wine 'library'), this is one to try – a simple café with bare stone walls, selling a huge range of wines, all reasonably priced and of excellent quality. The menu features lots of snacks and starters, designed to complement the wines. There are *crostini* with various toppings, plates of paper-thin salami or *prosciutto*, and a great choice of salads. It's an informal and easy-going place to taste a few noble Tuscan wines and eat a few Tuscan delicacies without spending a fortune. $

Croce al Trebbio
Via delle Belle Donne 47r
Tel: 055-287089
The restaurant lies one block east of Santa Maria Novella in a piazza so small it doesn't feature on maps. Called Croce del Trebbio, it is named after a Roman pillar, now topped with a cross and symbols of the Evangelists, marking the meeting of three streets (Trebbio is derived from the Latin *trivium* – 'three ways'). The restaurant serves excellent Tuscan *crostini*, seasonal salads, tripe (much better than it sounds), and grilled prawns – plus a good-value *menu della casa*. Choose between the bare stone and vaulted ceiling of the intimate cellar, or the big beams and fireplace of the main restaurant. $$

Gran Caffè San Marco
Piazza di San Marco 15r
Tel: 055 284 235
Packed at lunchtime with students from the nearby art academy and with visitors who have spent the morning at the Accademia gallery, the Gran Caffè San Marco is a cake

shop that also sells a huge range of pizzas by the slice, as well as pasta dishes and roast meats. You can eat in the mirrored, air-conditioned interior, but those in the know seek out the garden terrace at the rear, entered round the corner, 20 metres/yds down Via Camillo Cavour at No. 122r. $

Hemingway by Night
Piazza Piatellina 9r
Tel: 055-284781
This is the perfect place if you are hungry in the small hours and need to recharge your batteries. Hemingway by Night is so named because Hemingway was always on the prowl for food at night, looking for a 'clean well-lighted place'. It only opens between midnight and 7am, Tues–Fri, but it buzzes with hungry clubbers who love its help-your-self salad bar, bagels, mini-quiches, cheese-cakes, ice-creams and other tasty treats. $

Latini ✳✳
Via dei Palchetti 6r
Tel: 055-210916
You will probably have to join the queue to get into this sprawling, noisy restaurant where you eat at communal tables. The reward for this (relative) discomfort is good filling Tuscan food (especially the meat dishes) and the chance to make some new friends. Closed Monday, Tuesday lunch, all August and Christmas. $$

La Loggia
Piazzale Michelangelo
Tel: 055-234832
Set in an elegant 19th-century stone pavil-ion that was originally planned as an art gallery, La Loggia stands in gardens to the south of the square to which everyone loves to come for panoramic views over the city rooftops. Depending on your mood, your appetite and the time of day, you can indulge in ice-cream or sorbet, fresh fruit, coffee, cakes with sparkling wine, or classic Tuscan cuisine, in elegant surroundings. $$$

Da Mario
Via della Rosina 2r
Tel: 055-218550
Tucked away behind market stalls, this Flo-rentine *trattoria* has a lively atmosphere and

is popular with local stall holders. Closed in the evening, on Sunday and in August. $

Marione
Via della Spada 27r
Tel: 055-214756
A traditional *trattoria* just off Via Tornabuoni. Closed on Sunday and from mid-July to mid-August. $

Osteria Caterina de'Medici
Piazza del Mercato Centrale 12
Tel: 055-210620
Caterina de'Medici was the one who married Henri II of France in 1535 and was so appalled by French food that she brought her own cooks from Italy to teach the French how to cook – hence her sobriquet 'the mother of French cuisine'. The dishes at this smart restaurant live up to her name – whether you go for the extravagance of *far-falline alla Zarina* (salmon, vodka and caviar) or earthy *trippa alla fiorentina*, delicious braised tripe in a rich garlic and tomato sauce, topped with soft flakes of parmesan. $$

Osteria dei Centopoveri
Via Palazzuolo 31r
Tel: 055-218846
A tiny restaurant with a rustic atmosphere serving classic Tuscan and Pugliese dishes with a daily special of fish. Dishes are all prepared on the spot in the open kitchen and beautifully presented. Closed on Tuesday. $$

Right: pasta and salad – a simple but classic combination of tastes

Osteria di Santo Spirito
Piazza Santo Spirito 16r
Tel: 055-2382383
The position of this popular osteria is hard to beat; its terrace is right on beautiful piazza Santo Spirito. Popular with a young crowd, it serves an inventive menu which includes plenty of fish dishes. You can either have a light snack and a glass of wine or an elaborate meal. $–$$

Osteria No. 1
Via del Moro 22
Tel: 055-294318
In this street of artists' studios and antique shops is Gianni Giradi's elegant restaurant, decorated with original paintings and statues. All the usual Tuscan dishes are on the menu, plus such specials as richly flavoured, grilled *porcini* mushrooms, venison *(cervo)* in myrtle sauce, rabbit *(coniglio)* and duck breast *(petto d'anatra)* – plus truffles and fresh asparagus if you feel like really splashing out. $$

Pane e Vino
Via San Niccolò 70r
Tel: 055-2476956
Many people come for the imaginative, good-value daily set *menu degustazione* with six courses at this pleasant, informal restaurant. But if that is too much for you to handle, choose from other tempting dishes as well as a varied wine list. Open until midnight (rare in Florence). Closed at lunchtime and Sunday. $$

Enoteca Pinchiorri
Via Ghibellina 87
Tel: 055-242777
A gourmet paradise with a true connoisseur's wine list, hailed by some as one of the best restaurants in Europe and scorned by others as being pretentious and over-priced. Serves traditional Tuscan dishes and a more creative menu. There is a delightful courtyard for summer dining. Closed all day Sunday, Monday and Wednesday lunchtime and August; reservations essential. $$$+

Il Pizzaiuolo
Via de' Macci 113r
Tel: 055-241171
The name of this restaurant means 'pizza maker', and the various pizzas on offer here – all of which are Neapolitan-style with light, puffy bases – are wonderful. There is lots more besides, including a generous mixed *antipasto* and a good range of shellfish. This is a very popular establishment, so booking is recommended. $

Da Ruggero
Via Senese 89r
Tel: 055-220542
This is a small, old-fashioned *trattoria* on the Siena road near Porta Romana. Closed Tuesday and Wednesday. $

Ruth's
Via L C Farini 2a
Tel: 055-248 0888
This bright modern café next door to the synagogue serves kosher Middle Eastern food. Tempting daytime snacks include *brik* (filo pastry parcels oozing with soft cheese) and *imam bayildi* (aubergines stuffed with pine nuts and raisins), while the evening menu features grilled vegetables, fish couscous and Ruth's Platter – a selection of Middle Eastern specialities. Closed Friday from 2.30pm and Saturday till 7.30pm. $

Sostanza
Via del Porcellana 25r
Tel: 055-212691
Although this long-established *trattoria* – it was established in 1869 – is very plain and down-to-earth, it has in the past enjoyed the patronage of such famous guests as poet

Left: it is always important to leave room for dessert

menu, but the seafood *spaghetti allo Stefano* (which comes complete with bib) is a meal in itself. $$$

Totó

Borgo Santi Apostoli
Tel: 055-212096

A display of aged beef and the large scales for weighing out portions tells you that this cavernous vaulted restaurant specialises in *bistecca alla fiorentina*, grilled over the embers of a big open fire, which fills the dining room with wonderful woody scents. If steak isn't your thing, there are plenty of other delicious choices, including *cinghiale in umido* (wild boar in red wine sauce) and *sogliola alla mugnaia* (pan-fried sole in lemon butter). $$

Trattoria del Carmine

Piazza del Carmine 18r
Tel: 055-218601

This is a small *trattoria* situated in the 'Oltrarno' area. The daily specials and Tuscan soups are especially recommended. Offers some outside tables in the summer. Closed Sunday. $

Uffizi

Via dei Castellani 22r
Tel: 055-219520

There are plenty of second-rate restaurants in the vicinity of the Uffizi, so it's worth walking just a little further to this one, in the street to the east of the gallery, where this good, traditional *trattoria* decorated with bright modern paintings is located. The good-value *menu del giorno* (menu of the day) doesn't skimp on quality – truffle risotto, grilled prawns, and *porcini* all feature in the appropriate season. $$

Trattoria Za-Za

Piazza del Mercato Centrale 26r
Tel: 055 215411

Hearty food served in a riotous atmosphere, with such staples as *arrosto* (roast meat) and bean delicacies. It is very popular with tourists in the evening, but they are plagued by buskers who play at the tables and make a nuisance of themselves until they are paid to go away. However, it is still a good choice for lunch. Closed Sunday. $

Ezra Pound and Ronald Reagan (in his acting days). Equally famous is the *petto di pollo al burro*, chicken breast in butter. Closed Saturday and Sunday. $$

La Spada

Via del Moro 66r
Tel: 055-218 757

Heavy beams and Tiffany lamps, alcoves decorated with straw-wrapped Chianti bottles – it sounds like a caricature of an Italian restaurant, but locals flock here for the authentic and excellent-value special lunches. In the evening, as well as such standards as *ribolitta* and steak, you can try *fettunta con fagioli* – a superior version of beans on toast, made with garlic-flavoured white beans, boar sausage – *salsicce di cinghiale*. Finish your meal with homemade *zuccotto*, a decadent Florentine speciality consisting of rum-flavoured sponge cake wrapped around a creamy chocolate and almond centre. $$

Da Stefano

Via Senese 271, Galluzo
Tel: 055-2049105

It is worth making the short trip out of town to Galluzo (3km/2 miles south) to eat at Stefano's, widely considered to be the best fish restaurant in Florence. Stefano himself proudly guides you through the evening's

Above: locally made *biscotti* are delicious with coffee

NIGHTLIFE

Florence is basically a provincial town and its nightlife is relatively low-key and civilised. Florentines do not, on the whole, burn the night away in a frenetic trawl from one club or discotheque to another. Most of them favour a leisurely meal and a stroll round their city in the cool of the night. Entertainment venues divide between piano bars for the older generation and, for the young, discos, clubs and cafés. The nightly *passeggiata* between the two main piazzas is worth catching *(see page 59)*.

The tourist authority (APT) puts out a monthly poster – the *Calendario delle Manifestazione* (Calendar of Events) – which you will find displayed in most hotels; this is not a comprehensive guide, but it does list all the major coming events and your hotel concierge may be willing to phone and book tickets on your behalf (or you can apply to the central box-office, Via Alamanni 39 (tel: 055-210804).

Alternatively, the tourist information office at Via Cavour 1r (near the Palazzo Medici Riccardi, tel: 055-290832/33) has a noticeboard displaying details of the events that can be enjoyed by English-speaking visitors. This covers everything from films to jazz, rock and classical concerts, opera, dance and theatre. The staff at the tourist office are also happy to help make bookings on your behalf.

Bars and Clubs

Cafe Be Bop
Via dei Servi 76r
(no telephone)
Very young, jumpy place that doesn't come alive until 11pm. Live music most nights.

La Dolce Vita
Piazza del Carmine 6r
Tel: 055-284595
Fashionable, late-night bar. Hung with the work of local artists and photographers. Live music on Thursday. Closed Sunday.

Fiddler's Elbow
Piazza Santa Maria Novella 7r
Tel: 055-215056
Straight out of James Joyce's Dublin, an Irish bar with real character. Open 4pm–1am.

Giubbe Rosse
Piazza della Repubblica 13r
Tel: 212280
Named after the snazzy red jackets worn by

Above: the sun sets over the Ponte Vecchio

the waiters and historically a haunt of artists and intellectuals.

Jazz Club
Via Nuova de' Caccini 3
Tel: 055-2479700
Offers live jazz and good beers. Open Tues–Sat 9.30pm–2am.

Paszkowski
Piazza della Repubblica 31–35r
Tel: 055-210236
Grand piano bar (sometimes there is a small orchestra, too) playing light music; popular with those old enough to remember when the songs were new. Closed Mon.

Rex Caffè
Via Fiesolana 25r
Tel: 055-2480331
The Rex is a good, rambling bar popular with the younger artistic community in Florence. Tapas served 5–9.30pm.

Il Bordello
Via Tripoli 11r
Tel: 055-234849
A former brothel, this is now one of the best-known spots in Florence for laid-back late-night drinking. Has comfortable sofas, and 19th-century photos of nudes on the walls, and a mixed crowd of straights and gays. Open 5pm–6am

Rivoire
Piazza della Signoria 5r
Tel: 055-214412
Great views of the Palazzo Vecchio; the perfect place for a romantic evening, with good wine, cocktails, great ice-cream and pastries. Closed Mon and the last two weeks of Jan.

Cinemas
Two cinemas in Florence show the latest film releases on one day a week:

Goldoni
Via de' Serragli 109
Tel: 055-222437
Odeon
Via Sassetti 1
Tel: 055-214068

Right: robust Tuscan wines

Astro
Piazza San Simone (opposite Vivoli's ice cream shop in Via Isola delle Stinche, near Santa Croce)
No telephone
Shows exclusively English-language films six days a week, although they are not usually the newest releases. Shows at 7.30 and 10pm. Closed Mon.

Discos and Live Music
Lido
Lungarno Pecori Giraldi 1r
Tel: 055-2342726
With its riverside setting, the Lido is one of the most attractive discos in Florence. Open until 2am. Closed Mon and the whole of Jan and Feb.

Maracana
Via Faenza 4
Tel: 055-210298
Classy Latino club with salsa, samba and funky 1970s disco music. Open Tues–Sun midnight–4am.

Meccanò
Viale degli Olmi 1
Tel: 055-3313371
Mecannò is an enormous disco, Florence's most famous. In summer, the whole thing moves outdoors. Open Tues–Sat 11pm–6am.

Tenax
Via Pratese 47
Tel: 055-308160
This is the leading venue for arty, trendy Florentines. Mainly rock and new-wave music, but occasional live acts too. Open Wed–Sun 10pm till the early hours.

CALENDAR OF EVENTS

To experience Florence – and Tuscany – at its festive best, you need to spend the last two weeks of June or the first two weeks of August in and around the city – but make sure that you book your hotel well in advance, because lots of other people want to be here at these times too.

Information on events is not easy to come by far in advance – you really have to be there to find out what is going on. Most events are listed in *Firenze Spettacolo*, a comprehensive listings magazine, and also advertised around town by posters.

Some events are free, and you just turn up – for example, the fireworks spectacular that lights up the sky on Midsummer's Day (June 24), or the flag- throwing contests that you will suddenly find filling the Piazza della Signoria. Churches are busy with visiting choirs from Germany, the US and the UK performing for charity. Some museums (including the Archaeology Museum) open late and offer guided tours of parts not normally open to visitors.

There are indoor events – including grand opera at the Teatro Comunale – but in the sultry heat of the Florentine summer, it is better to be out of doors. The owners of some of the finest palaces in Florence open their gardens for charity : the admission price usually includes wine, refreshments and live chamber music.

Outdoor cinema screens are erected around town during the summer festivals, and several of the larger squares (including Santissima Annunziata and Santo Spirito) erect stages where free concerts are given every night after 9pm. The music on offer ranges from African bands touring Italy before going on to the WOMAD (World Music and Dance Festival) in the UK, to top blues guitarists, Beatles tribute bands and stars of the jazz world. Stalls spring up around the squares, selling wine, beer and Tuscan snacks.

Other top venues include the Roman theatre at nearby Fiesole, hosting the Florence Dance Festival – which has gone from strength to strength and now attracts the world's top modern dance companies; the Cathedral Square in Lucca, which rocks to the sounds of such artists as Mark Knopfler, Sting, or blues supremo Jeff Beck during a series of summer concerts.

Pistoia has a jazz festival at the same time, and there is a wonderful cross-over atmosphere as top-name musicians and complete unknowns mix informally and share music of the highest quality. The intimacy and small scale of many of these events are a major part of the appeal, along with ticket prices that are extremely reasonable compared to the cost of the average stadium rock event.

January–April

Music-lovers should check listings magazines to see what is on at the Teatro Pergola, Via della Pergola 18 (tel: 055-2479651); during the first three months of the year the Amici della Musica (Friends of Music) organise a programme of chamber concerts.
Shrove Tuesday: this is a low-key event in Florence, but nearby villages celebrate with fireworks and processions, the most notable of which are in Viareggio.
25 March: the normally tranquil Piazza della Santissima Annunziata comes alive to the sounds of excited children celebrating the feast of the Annunciation.
Easter: the **Scoppio del Carro** (Explosion of the Cart) takes place in the Piazza del Duomo and ostensibly celebrates the Resurrection, though pre-Christian fertility rites may actually underlie the custom. Crowds gather in the piazza to watch an 18th-century painted cart, in the shape of a tower, being drawn by white oxen to the Cathedral doors. If proceedings go according to plan, a rocket in the shape of a dove then swoops from the high altar through the Cathedral doors and ignites fireworks that are hidden in the carriage. The size and success of this conflagration serves as an omen indicating the likely outcome of that year's harvest.

May–July

Maggio Musicale (Musical May): the city's major arts festival is no longer confined to May, nor to music; concerts, classical and contemporary dance performances and opera are all now included and the events last through May and June and into July. Details

Right: Calcio in Costume in the Piazza di Santa Croce

of the festival can be obtained from Teatro Communale, Corso Italia 16, tel: 055-211158/213535, www.maggiofiorentino.com.

Estate Fiesolana (Fiesole Summer): this arts festival picks up the baton when Maggio Musicale tails off, with a celebration of music, drama and film from June to September. Most of the events take place in the Teatro Romana (Roman Theatre) in Fiesole, and at the Badia Fiesolana. Details are available from the tourist information office on Piazza Mino 36, Fiesole, tel: 055-5978372.

First Sunday after Ascension Day: the **Festa del Grillo** (Cricket Festival) can be seen as a religious festival or it can simply be regarded as a celebration of the joys of spring. Cascine Park, to the west of the city centre, fills with stalls selling crickets that are then released to ensure good luck.

Calcio in Costume: literally translated, this means 'Football in Costume' (the teams wear 16th-century dress) and it is held in June in Piazza Santa Croce. The game is played by four teams, representing the four original *rioni*, or districts, of the city. It is a cross between football and rugby, but there are few observable rules. Rivalry between the teams is intense and tactics are occasionally vicious. Each match is accompanied by a magnificent costumed procession which is well worth watching.

The game held on 24 June is the most spectacular because it coincides with Midsummer's Day and the Feast of St John the Baptist, the patron saint of Florence; celebrations last long into the night and there is a big firework display over the city, beginning at 10pm. Get a place on the north bank of the Arno for the best view.

Florence Dance Festival: an extravaganza of dancing in venues throughout the city takes place over three weeks in late June and early July. For further details of events, tel: 055-289276.

August–December

Festa della Rificolona (Lantern Festival): this is a low-key, but quite enchanting, festival that takes place on 7 September, the eve of the Birth of the Virgin. Children join in processions from all parts of the city, congregating in Piazza della Santissima Annunziata. They traditionally carry paper lanterns containing lighted candles.

During October and December: look out for chamber concerts at the Teatro della Pergola organised by the Amici della Musica.

Concerts: the Orchestra Regionale Toscana also gives concerts throughout the winter months in the Teatro Verdi and various other musical groups and orchestras perform in many of the city's other churches. The main opera season is September to December, with performances at the Teatro Comunale, Corso Italia 16.

Practical Information

GETTING THERE

By Air

The cheapest way to get to Florence is to fly to Pisa's Galileo Galilei Airport and take the train. Many airlines offer scheduled and charter flights to Pisa but advance reservations are essential, especially in the summer. The airport is more informal than most, yet efficient, and offers currency exchange, car rental, shopping and duty-free facilities. For information, tel: 050-500707.

To reach Florence from Pisa Aeroporto railway station, buy your train ticket at the information kiosk to the right of the customs exit at the airport. The railway station is located immediately to the left of the airport exit doors. Unfortunately, trains are not as frequent as you might expect and you might have to wait for a while. It is advisable to check that trains will be running if your flight arrives after 9pm.

An increasing number of European airlines now fly direct to Florence Peretola airport, 4km (2 miles) northwest of the city centre. You can also fly to Peretola from Milan, Rome and Venice, using Italy's domestic airline, Alitalia.

For airport information, tel: 055-373498; for flight information, tel: 055-3061702; e-mail: infoaeroporto@safnet.it

By Rail

The main railway station in Florence, Santa Maria Novella, is served by intercity and sleeper connections from all over Europe. Reservations are essential. Train fares may cost more than a cheap flight, unless you hold a rail pass that qualifies you for reduced fares. For rail information throughout Italy, tel: 1478-88088.

By Road

If you can bear the long, uncomfortable journey, there are plenty of coach services to Florence from European capitals. However, as is the case with travelling by train, you may find that flying is cheaper.

Travelling into Florence by car is not really recommended, because you will have problems once you arrive; traffic is banned from the historic centre and parking is very difficult. There are two large car parks in town, which are open 24 hours and day and have surveillance cameras. These are at the Parterre (near Piazza Libertà) and under the railway station. The former is considerably cheaper. The alternative is to use one of the numerous small private car parks in the city.

TRAVEL ESSENTIALS

When to Visit

Although Florence is an all-year-round destination, the heat and crowds of July and August are best avoided; the crowds and queues can also be unbearable at Easter. If you are visiting Florence for just a few days, try to avoid Sunday afternoon and Monday when many of the city's museums, shops and restaurants are closed. May is probably the best month to see Florence, but June, late September and October are also relatively cool and peaceful.

Left: checking times in the bus station
Right: a leisurely form of transport

November to March can be wetter and colder than you would believe possible in a Mediterranean climate but, to compensate, the city will be far less crowded and you will probably find bargain-price air fares and hotel rooms. If you want to visit Florence during the Calcio in Costume festival you would be wise to book at least six months in advance.

Visas and Passports

Nationals of the US, EU and Commonwealth countries need only an up-to-date passport to enter Italy. Other nationals should apply in advance for a visa from the nearest Italian consulate in their home country.

Vaccinations

No vaccinations required.

Customs

There are no currency limitations, either incoming or outgoing. Unpreserved meat products are not permitted; other unpreserved foodstuffs must be declared. Goods not incurring duties are:

EU: In principle there are no limits on goods on which duty has already been paid in the European country from which you have travelled. Travellers may need to prove that excessive amounts are for personal use only.

Non-EU: 200 cigarettes or 50 cigars or 250g tobacco; 2 litres still wine; either 1 litre of spirits or 2 litres sparkling or fortified wine; 50g perfume and 0.25 litres eau de toilette.

Weather and Clothing

Winter in Florence can be bitingly cold but is often clear and sunny, so the city looks marvellous, although you will need to wrap up to enjoy it. Winter can last until Easter and the short spring is often marked by heavy rain. Thereafter, temperatures rise rapidly to 25°C (78°F) or more from May to September. Florentines judge people very much on the basis of personal appearance so dress well, in smart casual clothes, rather than slumming it. September to November are the wettest months, when an umbrella and raincoat are indispensable.

What to Bring

Binoculars are useful if you want to study frescoes in detail, since many of them are located high up on church walls.

Electricity

The supply is 220 volts and sockets are for plugs of the standard mainland Europe type, with two round pins. You will need an adaptor to use British three-pin appliances and a transformer if the appliances normally

Above: catering to visitors' needs

operate at 100–120 volts (the US and Canadian standard).

Time

Italy observes Central European Time (one hour ahead of Greenwich Mean Time) and clocks change at the end of April and October, on the same day as in the UK.

MONEY MATTERS

Currency

Italy, in common with the other 10 countries of the Eurozone, switched to the euro on 28 February 2002, at which point the lira ceased to be legal tender. Euro banknotes are issued in denominations of €5, 10, 20, 50, 100, 200 and 500, and coins in denominations of €1 and 2, and cents 1, 2, 5, 10, 20 and 50.

Credit Cards

The major credit cards (Visa, MasterCard, American Express and Diners Club) are accepted in many hotels, restaurants and shops (look for a sign saying *Carta Si* – literally, 'Card Yes' – in the window).

Cash Machines

You can obtain cash from machines displaying a blue and red EC (Euro Card) sign using most of the major credit and debit cards, providing you know your pin number. The system is not infallible, however; if the machine swallows your card, you can usually retrieve it by presenting your passport to the bank within three days. Generally speaking, this is an expensive way of obtaining money, since you pay a handling charge of around 1.5 per cent and, on credit cards, interest is charged at a high rate from the moment you receive the cash; however, it is often quicker than cashing travellers' cheques and is useful in an emergency.

Several banks in Florence also have automatic exchange machines into which you can feed bank notes and receive euros in return. Instructions are given in several languages and the exchange rate is the same as that offered by banks; these machines are, however, apt to reject any notes that are creased or damaged.

Exchange

Travellers' cheques (obtainable in euros) are easy to cash, but remember that you will be required to present your passport. Banks offer the best rates and are normally open Monday to Friday from 8.20am–1.20pm. Some banks also open in the afternoon from 2.30pm–3.45pm. The Banco Nazionale at the railway station is open continuously from 8.20am–7.20pm Monday to Saturday. Outside these hours and at weekends you can use automatic exchange machines to change cash. Small exchange booths often charge up to 3 percent commission.

Tipping

Tips are not expected, but they are appreciated. Service charge is included in most restaurant bills but you may wish to leave a little extra for good service. Fifty cents is an adequate tip for taxi drivers and porters.

USEFUL INFORMATION

Geography and Economy

Florence is the capital of Tuscany and lies on the River Arno, 80km/50 miles inland from the sea. The Arno valley and the plain to the west of Florence are heavily built up and industrialised; glass-making, motorcycle manufacture, textiles and gold-working are among the major industries, as well as intensive horticulture and market-gardening.

Florence itself (pop: 500,000) is a major centre for artisan-based industries, e.g. *haute couture*, textile manufacture, leather-working and paper-making; in addition, it has a thriving service sector, which includes banking, legal services and insurance.

HEALTH AND EMERGENCIES

Pharmacies

A *farmacia* is identified by a cross, often red and usually in neon at night. The shops are staffed by trained pharmacists who can prescribe drugs, including antibiotics, that are only available by doctor's prescription in some other countries. Normal opening hours are Monday to Friday 9am–1pm and

4pm–7pm. The address of the nearest *farmacia* on emergency duty will be posted in chemists' windows. The Farmacia Comunale, at the railway station, is open all night.

Medical Services
In the event of an emergency, tel: 118 – the general emergency number. Every public hospital in Florence has a 24-hour casualty department *(Pronto Soccorso)* where treatment is free. The most central in Florence is the Ospedale Santa Maria Nuova, Piazza Santa Maria Nuova, tel: 055-27581. Otherwise, medical care has to be paid for. EU nationals should obtain form E111 from post offices or health and social security departments in advance of their visit and follow the instructions to obtain a reimbursement of

the costs. However, it is also advisable to take out travel insurance providing cover for emergency medical care.

Crime
Florence is a relatively safe city but pickpocketing is rife in certain areas, such as the market around San Lorenzo, the railway station and around Santa Maria Novella. Keep photocopies of important documents separately from the originals, to help the replacement process if they are lost or stolen. If you need to report a theft, go to the police station *(questura)* on Via Zara 2 (tel: 055-49771) and make a statement *(denuncia)* using an official, multilingual form, keeping one stamped copy for yourself for making an insurance claim.

The *Vigili Urbani* are traffic police whose main job is to prevent infringement of parking regulations and keep unauthorised vehicles out of the centre during prohibited hours. Local police matters are handled by the *Polizia*. If you need them in an emergency, dial 113. You may also see armed police – the *Carabinieri*; they are a national police force, technically a branch of the army, which deals with serious crime.

Toilets
Some museums have public toilets but elsewhere they scarcely exist. Toilets in bars are for customer use, so buy a coffee first and ask for the *bagno, toilette* or *gabinetto*. One toilet may serve for both sexes; otherwise they may be marked *signore* or *donne* for women and *signori* or *uomini* for men.

GETTING AROUND

Florence is so compact that you really can walk everywhere. You may, however, want to take the occasional taxi if you are carrying luggage or are out late at night. You will find taxi ranks at the railway station and in the following *piazze*: Santa Trinità, della Repubblica, del Duomo and San Marco. For a radio taxi, tel: 055-4390/4242/4798.

Buses
Buses in Florence are bright orange in colour and are run by ATAF. To save time trying to work out all the routes, simply remember that most buses pass through, and can be caught from, Piazza del Duomo or Santa Maria Novella station. Bus numbers and routes are clearly displayed at each bus-stop.

Tickets are not available on the bus and must be bought in advance from bars and tobacco shops displaying the ATAF sticker. You will also find a ticket kiosk and ticket-dispensing machines in the street alongside main bus-stops. The ticket should be fed into the stamping machine at the rear of the bus

Above: a red cross indicates a chemist
Right: signs at bus stops show the routes

on entry. Each ticket is valid for 60 minutes' travel, during which time you can change from one bus to another as often as you like. It is also possible to buy 3-hour and 24-hour tickets.

Maps and Guides

The map in the back of this guide is likely to fulfil most of your needs; it plots the itineraries found in the Places of this guide and includes a gazetteer to help you locate streets listed in the shopping, eating out and nightlife sections. For a durable, all-weather map, look out for Insight Guides' laminated *Flexi Map: Florence*. For a very detailed map of the city, look for *Firenze: Pianta della Citta*, published by LAC (Litografia Artistica Cartografica).

Of the guidebooks currently available, *Insight Guide: Florence* (Apa Publications) includes features that get beneath the skin of the Florentines. Most museums in Florence sell excellent illustrated guides to their own collections.

Tourist Offices

The main office is at Via Manzoni 16 but this is a long way out of the city centre and is only open to the public in the morning (9am–1pm, closed Sun). Much more useful are the three branch offices in the centre. One is located near Piazza Santa Croce (Borgo Santa Croce 29r, tel: 055-2340444) while the second is near the Medici-Riccardi

Palace (Via Cavour 1r, tel: 055-290832) and the third is at Piazza Stazione (tel: 055-212245). They are available to personal callers only (no telephone service) and are usually open daily 9am–7pm.

ACCOMMODATION

Hotels

Hotels in Italy are graded and priced on a one- to five-star system according to their facilities. This is no indication of their atmosphere. Florence is surpassed only by Venice in terms of the price of accommodation; it is a very expensive place to stay. Cheap hotels do exist (especially near the station along Via Nazionale and Via Faenza), but they are likely to be pretty shabby and almost all overlook noisy streets. Most decent hotels are in the three-star category and above, and you must be prepared to pay for them. However, many of these are in grand, historic buildings, and if you are lucky, you will find a roof terrace or garden, a huge bonus in hotter months. It is always advisable to book ahead, especially at Easter, Christmas and summer holiday periods and during the trade fairs in January and July. Many hotels cut their prices in low season (which often includes August), and it is worth bargaining. There is a room-reservation agency (the ITA) at the railway station which is open daily 9am–8pm to personal callers.

Above: the police find it easy to get around the city on horseback

Prices categories (for a double room):
$ = under €100; $$ = €100–150; $$$ = €150–230; $$$$ = over €230.

Brunelleschi

Piazza Santa Elisabetta 3
Tel: 055-27370; fax: 055-219653
info@hotelbrunelleschi.it
www.hotelbrunelleschi.it
A Byzantine tower (once a prison), and medieval church form part of this comfortable hotel located in a tiny central piazza. Two penthouse suites have 360-degree views of the city. $$$$

Excelsior

Piazza Ognissanti 3
Tel: 055-2715; fax: 055-210278
marco-milocco@westin.com
www.starwood.com
Old-world grandeur combined with modern conveniences; polished service, luxurious rooms (some of them with river views) and a roof-garden. Private parking. $$$$

Gallery

Vicolo del' Oro 5
Tel; 055-27263; fax 055-268557
gallery@lungarnohotels.com
www.lungarnohotels.com
Brand new boutique hotel a stone's throw from the Ponte Vecchio with minimalist designer interiors. Luxurious bedrooms and bathrooms. $$$$

Helvetia & Bristol

Via dei Pescioni 2
Tel: 055-287814; fax: 055-288353
reservation_hbf@charminghotels.it
www.charminghotels.it
One of the best small hotels in Florence; very central and grand but not stuffy. The public rooms are full of antiques and paintings; the bedrooms are sumptuous. Winter garden and gourmet restaurant. $$$$

Kraft

Via Solferino 2
Tel: 055-284 273; fax: 055-239 8267
info@krafthotel.it
www.krafthotel.it
Located almost opposite the city's Teatro Comunale opera house, so staying here will allow you to rub shoulders with visiting singers, conductors and wealthy music lovers. The hotel has a large roof garden and a swimming pool – rare features that make the Kraft well worth the extra expense. $$$$

Lungarno

Borgo San Jacopo 14
Tel: 055-27261; fax: 055-268437
lungarnohotels@lungarnohotels.com
www.lungarnohotels.com
Smart, comfortable modern hotel, very popular for its superb position on the river and its views of the Ponte Vecchio from the front rooms. Restaurant specialising in fish; private parking. $$$$

Above: the Pensione Alessandra is central and moderately priced

Albion
Via Il Prato 22r
Tel: 055-214 171, fax: 055-283 391
info@hotelalbion.it
www.hotelalbion.it
This delightful hotel in a 19th-century 'palazzo-villa' is near the Teatro Comunale opera house in the city's south-western suburbs. Designed by the Milanese sculptor, Ignazio Villa, the palace is a fine example of English neo-Gothic architecture. Pointed arches feature everywhere – in windows, bedheads and designs on carpets and textiles. The basement has been turned into a library full of books about the history and artistic treasures of Florence. Bicycles are provided for guests so you can park your car in the hotel garage and enjoy getting around the green and healthy way. $$$

Beacci Tornabuoni
Via de'Tornabuoni 3
Tel: 055-212645; fax: 055-283594
info@bthotel.it
www.bthotel.it
A distinctly old-fashioned feel pervades this hotel set in a 14th-century palazzo with roof-garden in the city's most prestigious shopping street. Private parking. $$$

Casa Guidi
Piazza San Felice
Tel: 01628-825925, fax: 01628-825417
bookings@landmarktrust.co.uk
www.landmarktrust.co.uk
The Florentine home of 19th-century poets Elizabeth and Robert Browning is now available for letting by the night or by the week through the Landmark Trust, a UK-based charity that rescues and restores historic buildings as holiday lets. The nightly cost of renting the apartment is similar to that of an upmarket hotel, but here you get six beds right in the heart of Florence, as well as grand and romantic rooms, furnished with Renaissance paintings, antiquarian books, a grand piano and 18th-century furnishings. $$$

Grand Hotel Baglioni
Piazza dell' Unità Italiana 6
Tel: 055-23580; fax: 055-2358895
info@hotelbaglioni.it
www.hotelbaglioni.it
This clasic hotel is especially popular with the business community. It is discreetly elegant, with comfortable rooms and good service. The roof-top restaurant has fabulous views of the city. $$$

Il Guelfo Bianco
Via Cavour 57r
Tel: 055-288330; fax: 055-295203
info@ilguelfobianco.it
www.ilguelfobianco.it
Il Guelfo Bianco offers comfortably furnished rooms in two adjacent 15th-century houses just north of the Duomo. The family rooms are very spacious and there is also a little courtyard. $$$

Hermitage
Vicolo Marzio 1, Piazza del Pesce
Tel: 055-287216; fax: 055-212208
florence@hermitagehotel.com
www.hermitagehotel.com
Delightful hotel with a lovely roof garden in a hidden piazza with views over the Ponte Vecchio. Some of the (rather small) rooms have river views, although the quieter ones at the back do not. $$$

J&J
Via di Mezzo 20
Tel: 055-263121; fax: 055-240282
jandj@dada.it
www.jandjhotel.com
Housed in a former convent near Sant' Ambrogio, this smart, discreet hotel is interior designed throughout. Breakfast is served in the cloister in summer. The rooms (some of which are absolutely huge) are comfortable. $$$

Loggiato dei Serviti
Piazza della Santissima Annunziata 3
Tel: 055-289592; fax: 055-289595
loggiato_serviti@italyhotel.com
www.venere.it/firenze/loggiato_serviti
Loggiato dei Serviti is one of Florence's most refined small hotels, occupying a splendid 16th-century *palazzo*. It stands in a beautiful traffic-free *piazza* and offers views onto Brunelleschi's Ospedale degli Innocenti. Antiques adorn the vaulted interior and the bedrooms are all beautifully and individually decorated. $$$

Torre di Bellosguardo
Via Roti Michelozzi 2
Tel: 055-2298145; fax: 055-229008
torredibellosguardo@dada.it
www.members.aol.com/puterbugzz/
tbellos.html
Set in the hills above Porta Romana, this atmospheric hotel is composed of a 14th-century tower attached to a 16th-century villa. The frescoed reception rooms and individualistic bedrooms are studded with antiques and original features. Secluded swimming pool and delightful gardens. $$$

Villa Belvedere
Via B Castelli 3
Tel: 055-222 501; fax: 223 163
hotelvillabelvedere@tiscalinet.it
www.villabelvedere.com
Swap the noisy, cramped streets of Florence for the rural idyll of a fine villa set in spacious grounds just a little out of the centre of town. The Villa Belvedere lives up to its name in offering good views of the Tuscan hills south of the city. There are 15 spacious rooms with private bathrooms. The hotel has its own small pool, tennis courts and car park, and a magnificent indoor restaurant as well as a patio dining area, where home-made food is served using locally sourced ingredients. You could also sign up for the hotel's cookery courses and learn how to create authentic Tuscan dishes, from 10am–12.30pm every day. $$$

Villa Betania
Vialle del Poggio Imperiale 23
Tel/fax: 055-222 243
info@villabetania.it
www.villabetania.com
The Villa Betania is an old Medici-era villa located in one of the most exclusive areas of Florence – in the leafy villa and embassy district south of the Porta Romana. Surrounded by a beautiful garden, the villa feels rural but is only 1.5km (1 mile) from the Ponte Vecchio. The 15 spacious pastel-painted rooms have recently been superbly refurbished and now offer elegant accommodation at prices that compare very favourably with many cramped and noisy city-centre hotels. Prices include buffet breakfast and parking. $$$

Alessandra
Borgo SS Apostoli 17
Tel: 055-283438; fax: 055-210619
info@hotelalessandra.com
www.hotelalessandra.com
A central *pensione* with rooms ranging from quite grand with antique furniture to the more banal without bathroom. $$

Annalena
Via Romana 34
Tel: 055-222407; fax: 055-222403
annalena@hotelannalena.it
www.hotelannalena.it
Antique-furnished rooms in a gracious 15th-century former convent, built as a refuge for the widows of the Florentine nobility. Near the Boboli Gardens with views over a pretty nursery garden. $$

Aprile
Via della Scala 6
Tel: 055-216237; fax: 055-280947
aprile@italyhotel.com
More appealing than most hotels near the station, this is an ex-Medici palace with frescoes, a pleasant breakfast room and a garden. Rooms range from simple to quite grand and prices vary accordingly. $$

Botticelli
Via Taddea 8
Tel: 055-290905; fax: 055-294322
botticelli@fi.flashnet.it
www.panoramahotelsitaly.com
An appealing new hotel at the back of the central market. All mod cons plus original architectural features such as vaulted ceilings and the odd fresco. $$

Classic Hotel
Viale Machiavelli 25
Tel: 055-229351; fax: 055-229353
An attractive, pink-washed villa set in a shady garden on a tree-lined avenue just above Porta Romana. Rooms are spacious and comfortable with antique furniture. $$

Morandi alla Crocetta
Via Laura 50
Tel: 055-2344747; fax: 055-2480954
welcome@hotelmorandi.it
www.hotelmorandi.it

A quiet, informal hotel with only 10 rooms, housed in an ex-convent. Rooms are comfortable and furnished with some antiques; several have private terraces. $$

Splendor
Via San Gallo 30
Tel: 055-483427; fax: 055-461276
info@hotelsplendor.it
www.hotelsplendor.it
This small yet imposing *palazzo* near San Marco has surprisingly grand public rooms. Some of the bedrooms are rather shabby, but the leafy terrace is attractive. $$

Torre Guelfa
Borgo SS Apostoli 8
Tel: 055-2396338; fax: 055-2398577
torre.guelfa@flashnet.it
With the tallest privately owned tower in Florence; you can sip an *aperitivo* up there in the evenings. The bedrooms are pretty and equipped with smart bathrooms. $$

Bellettini
Via dei Conti 7
Tel: 055-213561; fax: 055-283551
hotel.bellettini@dada.it
www.firenze.net/hotelbellettini
Close to San Lorenzo market, this is an exceptionally friendly hotel with rooms decorated in simple Florentine style. $

Brunetti
Borgo Pinti 5, 3rd floor
Tel: 055-247 8134
Basic but clean one-star *albergo*. Unlike many budget hotels, this one has the merit of being on a relatively traffic-free street with no pubs or nightclubs in the vicinity – an essential prerequisite for a sound night's sleep. $

Casci
Via Cavour 13
Tel: 055-211686; fax: 055-2396461
casci@italyhotel.com
www.hotelcasci.com
A family-run hotel with a friendly atmosphere, the Casci occupies a frescoed *quattrocento palazzo* near the San Lorenzo market which once belonged to Rossini. All bedrooms are air-conditioned. $

Right: a welcome sign when you are looking for somewhere to stay

Firenze
Via del Corso/Piazza dei Donati 4
Tel: 055-268301; fax: 055-212370
A centrally located hotel with clean, functional rooms; all have private bathrooms. $

Montreal
Via della Scala 43
Tel: 055-238 2331; fax: 055-287 491
info@hotelmontreal.com
www.hotelmontreal.com
One of the cheapest hotels in Florence, and only a short distance from the station, so not far to lug bags, or stagger for an early morning train. The hotel is simple and clean, but whether your stay is heaven or hell depends on which room you get: those at the front suffer from the noise of nearby bars and restaurants, especially in summer when you need the windows open for air. $

Palazzo Vecchio
Via B. Cennini 4
Tel: 055-212182; fax: 055-216445
info@hotelpalazzovecchio.it
www.hotelpalazzovecchio.it
A pleasant, comfortable and modern hotel right opposite the station, with good facilities for the price. All rooms have private bathrooms. Free car parking. $

La Scaletta
Via Guicciardini 13
Tel: 055-283028; fax: 055-289562
lascaletta.htl@dada.it
www.lascaletta.com

Not all the rooms in this hotel near the Pitti Palace have private bathrooms and some are dowdy. However, there is a lovely roof garden with panoramic views over Florence. Half board available. $

Tina
Via San Gallo 31
Tel: 055-483 519, fax: 055-483 593
hoteltina@tin.it
This friendly hotel is a great favourite with young visitors: a cross between an upmarket youth hostel and a low-cost hotel, it is welcoming to all-comers, straight or gay, and offers clean basic comfort in a not-too-noisy part of town to the north of the ever-popular San Lorenzo market. $

Toscana
Via del Sole 8
Tel/fax: 055-213 156
h.toscana@dada.it
www.hoteltoscana.it
If luxury hotel frills don't thrill you, try this small hotel offering four single and seven double rooms, all with private bathrooms in the city centre at very reasonable prices; breakfast included. $

Camping
Camping di Fiesole
Via Peramondo 1
Tel: 055-599 069
If you want to camp or park a camper van, this campsite in the cool wooded Fiesole hills is the best of the options available around Florence. The campsite is clean and well run, but it is very busy in the height of the summer, especially in August and is a 15-minute walk or so from the bus stop in Fiesole's main square. $

Camping Italiani e Stranieri
Viale Michelangiolo 88
Tel: 055-681 1977
On the south side of the city, this site is popular with young people and is often noisy until the early hours of the morning. $

HOURS AND HOLIDAYS

Opening Hours
Shops: summer: Monday to Saturday **9am–1pm** and **4–8pm**; winter: Monday to Saturday **9am–1pm** and **3.30–7.30pm**. Some shops close on Monday, or at least in the morning. Flower and cake shops open in the morning on Sunday and public holidays, when Florentines like to treat themselves and each other, but little else operates then, although bars remain open all day, every day. Many businesses, including restaurants, close for two weeks in August, the traditional holiday month in Italy.
Museums and Monuments: specific information on opening hours is given in the itinerary section of this book, but the opening hours are notoriously subject to change at short notice. Many hotels keep a list of the latest opening times for their guests to consult, so check before you set out and remember that most museums are closed on Monday. Churches are usually open 7am–1pm and from 4–7pm (or dusk in winter).

Public Holidays
Most businesses are closed on the following national holidays:
January 1
January 6 (Epiphany)
Good Friday
Easter Monday
April 25 (Liberation Day)
May 1 (Labour Day)
August 15 (Assumption)
November 1 (All Saints)
December 8 (Immaculate Conception)
December 25 and 26 (Christmas)
In addition to these public holidays, many businesses close on and around June 24, when

Above: Florentines like to relax in the middle of the day

the city celebrates the feast of its patron saint, St John the Baptist. August is the official holiday month in Italy when some shops and restaurants will be closed.

MEDIA

You will have no difficulty in buying the major European newspapers, although you may find they arrive a day late. If you are literate in Italian, the daily *La Nazione* and *La Repubblica* contain details of local entertainment and events.

Cultural events are listed in English-language listings magazines, generally available in hotels or from tourist information offices, entitled *Florence Today* and *Florence Concierge Information*. There is also an English section in the monthly listings magazine *Firenze Spettacolo*.

POST AND TELECOMMUNICATIONS

Tobacconists sell postage stamps for letters and postcards: look for a sign with the white letter T on a black background. For other transactions go to the central post office (Palazzo delle Poste) at Via Pelliceria 3, near Piazza della Repubblica, open Monday to Friday, 8.15am–7pm and Saturday 8.15am–12.30pm.

Coin-operated phones can be found in many streets and squares; you can phone from a bar if it displays the sign of a red telephone handset in a red circle. Insert the coins before you dial and add more if you hear a beep. Many public phones accept phone cards *(carta telefonica)* that can be bought in tobacconists.

Telephone booths for long-distance or overseas calls are located in the central post office (open 24 hours, Via Pelliceria 160) and the railway station (open Monday to Saturday 8am–9.45pm). Here you can make metered calls and pay afterwards by cash or credit card, which is much more convenient. To get an international line, dial 00.

When dialling any number you must include the area code. The code for Florence is 055, and you must always include this number, even if you are dialling from within the city. You should also include the initial zero, even when you are dialling from outside Italy.

The engaged tone consists of a series of rapid pips; the dialling tone is a series of longer notes. When Italians answer the phone they say *pronto* (meaning 'ready').

FACILITIES FOR THE DISABLED

Facilities for people with disabilities in Italy in general are not good, and those in Florence are no exception. However, an increasing number of hotels have adapted rooms and bathrooms (although this does not mean that access to them will be good), and an increasing number of museums and galleries have lifts and ramps. There is a useful publication (written in Italian and English) available from the tourist office called *Museums and Monuments of Florence*, which describes accessibility to these places in detail.

All of the pavements in the centre of the city were levelled off at street corners in 2000, to allow wheelchair access. To obtain help if you wish to travel by train, tel: 055-2352275 or 055-2352533.

FURTHER READING

Of the many good books about Florence, Mary McCarthy's *The Stones of Florence and Venice Observed* (Penguin) is the most stimulating, but it does assume a considerable knowledge of the cities. As basic primers, try J.R. Hale's *Florence and the Medici* (Thames and Hudson); Irving Stone's *The Agony and the Ecstasy*; Penguin's *The Portable Renaissance Reader*; or Christopher Hibbert's *The Rise and Fall of the House of Medici* (Penguin).

Insight Guide: Florence (Apa Publications, 2000) and *Insight Guide: Tuscany* (Apa Publications, 2002) are fully illustrated guides providing in-depth essays, detailed coverage of the sights, excellent maps and up-to-date practical information. The latest addition to Insight's titles on Florence is the highly recommended *Insight Guide to Museums, Galleries and Churches of Florence* (Apa Publications, 2002).

INSIGHT
Pocket Guides

Insight Pocket Guides pioneered a new approach to guidebooks, introducing the concept of the authors as "local hosts" who would provide readers with personal recommendations, just as they would give honest advice to a friend who came to stay. They also included a full-size pull-out map. Now, to cope with the needs of the 21st century, new editions in this growing series are being given a new look to make them more practical to use, and restaurant and hotel listings have been greatly expanded.

ACKNOWLEDGEMENTS

Photography by

2/3, 20, 22, 23, 24T&B, 26, 27T, 29, 36, **Jerry Dennis**
37T&B, 38, 39T, 41, 43T&B, 44T, 47,
49T, 51, 53T&B, 60, 72, 73, 74, 75, 83, 84,
89, 90, 92B, 93, 98

15, 25, 34, 42, 46, 59B, 62, 63, 64, 65, 66, **Guglielmo Galvin & George Taylor**
67T&B, 69T&B, 70, 71, 76, 78, 79, 82
52B, 53, 55, 56, 58, 67, 68, 69, 70, 71, 87

12T&B, 16, 21, 27B, 28, 32T&B, 35, 44B, **Frances Gransden**
49B, 54, 55, 56, 57, 61, 88, 92T, 94, 97,
back cover

14 **Hans Höfer**
1, 8/9, 39B, 50,58, 59T, 77, 81, 85, 87, **Robert Mort**
Front cover **John Heseltine**
Cartography **Maria Donnelly**

© APA Publications GmbH & Co. Verlag KG Singapore Branch, Singapore

INDEX